KNOWLEDGE TRANSFER AND INNOVATION

This book demonstrates how managers can use and transfer knowledge more effectively to stimulate innovation in their organization in order to increase their competitive advantage.

Jones and Mahon draw on their discussions with combat Veterans, whose very survival relies on their skill in transferring crucial knowledge and information quickly, effectively and efficiently. They note that in today's competitive and fast-paced business world, these skills translate into continual innovation, metamorphosis and ultimately success. The authors have built a conceptual framework that demonstrates to the reader how to develop the same underlying skills and to use them effectively in the business environment.

With rich and lively examples throughout, *Knowledge Transfer and Innovation* equips students and practitioners of knowledge management, innovation, leadership and strategy with the skills, tools and strategies to succeed in today's fast-paced business environment.

Nory B. Jones is a Professor of Management Information Systems at the University of Maine, USA, where she focuses on knowledge management and e-business. Her research on knowledge transfer, the impact of social media on economic development, and entrepreneurship within the Veteran community has been featured in several journals around the globe.

John F. Mahon is a Professor of Management and the John M. Murphy Chair of International Business Policy and Strategy at the University of Maine, USA. He is a consultant for several international organizations and the author of numerous articles, cases and books.

"Excellent read and a wonderful tribute to our Veterans! Drs Jones and Mahon provide exceptional insight into the power of knowledge management and innovation through historical case studies, extensive interviews with military leaders and real world business examples. The book is a must have resource for leaders in any organization who want to enhance the power of their knowledge base and create the type of innovation needed for long term success. Great book for any leader's toolkit!"

—Brigadier General Rob Carmichael, *Maine Army National Guard*

"'If only we knew what we know' is a common lament in large organizations like the U.S. military. This book gives such organizations the tools to connect knowledge and put it to work for innovation and better performance."

—Thomas H. Davenport, *Babson College, Author of* Competing on Analytics

"In order to innovatively move forward, we must remain mindful of what has worked – or not worked – previously. Whether in business, the military, or as individuals, our ability to both gather and, often more importantly, use knowledge to our advantage is critical. *Knowledge Transfer and Innovation* provides a keen insight on turning knowledge into success, highlighting how to creatively tackle even the most daunting situations. A wonderful reminder of the deep, yet tenuous, connection between the past and the future."

—Robert Montgomery-Rice, *President and CEO, Bangor Savings Bank*

"Effective knowledge transfer is integral to the success of both a company and a battalion, and is the raison d'etre of a University. This book provides plenty to think about whether you are a professor, a captain of industry, or a Marine Corps tank commander."

—Dr. Robert Strong, *University of Maine*

KNOWLEDGE TRANSFER AND INNOVATION

Nory B. Jones and John F. Mahon

NEW YORK AND LONDON

First published 2018
by Routledge
711 Third Avenue, New York, NY 10017

and by Routledge
2 Park Square, Milton Park, Abingdon, Oxon, OX14 4RN

Routledge is an imprint of the Taylor & Francis Group, an informa business

© 2018 Taylor & Francis

The right of Nory B. Jones and John F. Mahon to be identified as
author of this work has been asserted by them in accordance with
sections 77 and 78 of the Copyright, Designs and Patents Act 1988.

All rights reserved. No part of this book may be reprinted or
reproduced or utilised in any form or by any electronic, mechanical,
or other means, now known or hereafter invented, including
photocopying and recording, or in any information storage or
retrieval system, without permission in writing from the publishers.

Trademark notice: Product or corporate names may be trademarks
or registered trademarks, and are used only for identification and
explanation without intent to infringe.

Library of Congress Cataloging in Publication Data
A catalog record for this title has been requested

ISBN: 978-1-138-71246-1 (hbk)
ISBN: 978-1-138-71247-8 (pbk)
ISBN: 978-1-315-20016-3 (ebk)

Typeset in Bembo
by Swales & Willis Ltd, Exeter, Devon, UK
Printed by CPI Group (UK) Ltd, Croydon CR0 4YY

CONTENTS

List of Illustrations	*vi*
Preface	*vii*
Acknowledgments	*viii*

1	Knowledge? What Knowledge?	1
2	Explosive Innovation: Putting Knowledge to Work	14
3	Leadership	32
4	Culture	50
5	Knowledge Corruption	65
6	Training and Socialization	87
7	Knowledge Structure and Processes	105
8	Technologies and Social Media	122
9	Putting It All Together	139
10	A "Rosetta Stone" for Military Skills Translation to Business	144

Index	*148*

ILLUSTRATIONS

Figures

1.1	Visualization of Knowledge	1
1.2	The Maginot Line	5
1.3	Example of Knowledge Flow	10
1.4	The Relationship of Tacit Knowledge Development and Performance	11
1.5	Relationships of Variables in Tacit Knowledge Transfer and Potential Knowledge Corruption	12
2.1	Nonaka's Knowledge Spiral	25
4.1	Cameron and Quinn's Organizational Culture Types	56
5.1	Knowledge Transfer	69
5.2	Knowledge Transfer Options	70
6.1	Learning from the Military—Continual Training Model	98
7.1	Knowledge Portal Model	106
7.2	Example of a Taxonomy	111
7.3	Example of an Organization's Ontology	113
8.1	The Internet of Things	129

Tables

7.1	Example of a Tourism Business Taxonomy in the Form of a Site Map	112
7.2	Example of a Marketing Agency Taxonomy in the Form of a Site Map	113

PREFACE

The puzzle of knowledge transfer and resulting innovation is complicated with many moving pieces. In this book, with the help of the Veterans we have spoken to at length, we break it down into the major components to identify crucial elements that are needed to recognize and gain knowledge, to share it and to use it effectively, resulting in the creation of new knowledge and innovation. We want to, as much as possible, avoid jargon and approaches that use difficult, academic and obtuse language. The U.S. military has spent countless resources on how to do this for strategic advantage—often representing the difference between life or death on the battlefield. For them, it is not a question of being competitive, but of outsmarting smart, evolving, ruthless enemies like the Taliban or ISIS in constantly changing environments. For our businesses, innovation similarly can represent the difference between success, survival, or the death of the organization. Thus, the lessons learned from these experienced Veterans along with best practices and lessons learned throughout history provides a foundation for success in our businesses today.

ACKNOWLEDGMENTS

We would like to thank the wonderful Veterans who took the time to share their valuable knowledge and experiences with us. We would also like to thank our spouses for their limitless support and encouragement: Gaylen Jones and Julie Mahon!

Veterans

Joshua Brown; Army, Iraq: SPC, U.S. Army. SPC Brown enlisted in the infantry and was deployed in Iraq. During his deployment, he also served as a radio operator and a cultural liaison, assisting officers in meetings with local tribal leaders.

Sean Christensen; Marines, Afghanistan: Retired Captain, December 2017, served 20 years with two combat tours in Afghanistan (Operation Enduring Freedom). Served as an Assistant Operations Officer in support of retrograde effort (collision forces' withdrawal) in Southern Helmand Province (2012) and as an Advisor to the Afghan National Army in Southern Helmand Province (2013-2014). Five Navy and Marine Corps Commendation Medals, two Navy and Marine Corps Achievement Medals. Infantry Mortarman, Infantry Platoon Sergeant and Logistics Officer.

Tyler Emery; Navy Corpsman, Iraq and Afghanistan: T.E. was a Navy Corpsman, embedded with combat Marine units. He served with the Marines in three deployments: one in Iraq and two in Afghanistan. His perspectives provided

Acknowledgments **ix**

valuable insights on crucial knowledge sharing during life and death situations in combat and saving the lives of people during and after combat missions.

Nathan Fry; Army, Afghanistan: Captain, U.S. Army, Operation Enduring Freedom: Served for seven years on active duty as an Infantry and MI Officer with the 2nd Infantry Division and 1st Armor Division. Served as Platoon Leader, Assistant Battalion Operations Officer and Battalion Intelligence Officer. Currently serves as a Company Commander with A/3-172 Infantry Regiment (Mountain), Vermont Army National Guard. Areas of notable experience include military mountaineering, arctic/cold weather operations and operational design.

SSG Keith Gauthier; Army, Iraq: Sergeant Gauthier was deployed to Iraq and provided valuable insights into how the Army shared knowledge and information both during deployment as well as during training and preparation for deployment.

Charles Knowlen; Army, Vietnam: Retired LT COL 1978, served 20 years with two years combat duty in Vietnam, Silver Star, Senior Aviator, Parachutist.

Robert E. La Brie; Army, Vietnam: Retired MSG from the U.S. with 22 years' service, two tours in Vietnam, two tours in Korea, awards include three Bronze Stars, The Meritorious Service Medal, Air Medal (5th Oak Leaf Cluster), Army Commendation Medal with 2nd Oak Leaf Cluster W/V device for Heroism, Purple Heart, Good Conduct Medal (5th award.)

Paul Lucey; Marines, World War II and Korea: World War II: Fighter pilot (Corsair) in Okinawa. Korea: Rescue helicopter pilot; after the wars; 31 years in the Marine Corps reserves, retired as Colonel, Distinguished Flying Cross and other medals.

Joseph Miller; Army, Iraq: Captain, Bronze Star Medal, Combat Infantry Badge, Global War on Terror Expeditionary Forces Medal, Iraqi Freedom Campaign Medal with Three Service Stars, Ranger Tab and Senior Parachutist Wings.

Matthew Murphy; Army, Afghanistan: Served 10 years in the military with combat tour in Afghanistan (Operation Enduring Freedom). Served in multiple direct action and collection capacities in various regions.

Norman Rossignol; Army, World War II and Korea: SSGT Retired after 20 years of service, 1964. World War II: 94th ID, Battle of the Bulge, two Bronze Stars (one pinned on by General Patton); Purple Heart; Combat Infantry Badge,

x Acknowledgments

European Theatre, four Stars; Korea: 25th ID, Korean Service Medal, two Stars; United Nations Medal, Good Conduct Medal.

LTC Jeffery Shirland; Army, Afghanistan and Kuwait: LTC Shirland was deployed to Afghanistan and Kuwait and provided valuable insights into how the Army shared knowledge and information both during deployment as well as during training and preparation for deployment.

Joseph Swoboda; Army, Iraq: Retired SFC. 3rd Infantry Division, Operation Iraqi Freedom—1, 3 and 5. 1st Army unit to earn the Combat Action Badge, Bronze Star Medal for meritorious service at Objective Peach Battle of the Euphrates.

1
KNOWLEDGE? WHAT KNOWLEDGE?

> Gaining knowledge, is the first step to wisdom.
> Sharing it is the first step to humanity.
>
> —*Author Unknown*

What is knowledge and why is it important? "Knowledge is power" and valuable knowledge, when used correctly, in a timely manner and at the appropriate level, can save lives in the battlefield or result in success in the business world. Consider the visual representation of "knowledge" in Figure 1.1 below. Please note that you can substitute "organization" for "I" here.

In Circle A, we find true ignorance. In this particular state for either an individual or an organization, there is no knowledge of what is unknown, and as such no questions can be asked or explorations undertaken. When we migrate to Circle B (as shown by the number 1) we have made a significant leap . . . we now know what we know and can therefore ask questions and explore and advance

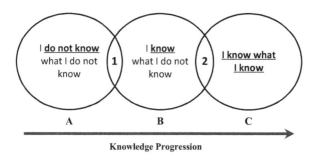

FIGURE 1.1 Visualization of Knowledge

2 Knowledge? What Knowledge?

our knowledge. But let us be clear here, this is a choice and an *action* step. Many individuals and organizations stop here—they are comfortable in "knowing" what they do not know, but do not wish to pursue answers or knowledge or understanding. In Circle C the individual or organization has acted on what it has found out in Circle B and obtained knowledge—the organization or the individual now "knows" and has actionable and useful knowledge. According to futurists Talwar and Lazarova (undated),

> An individual's professional knowledge is becoming outdated at a much faster rate than ever before. Rapid changes in the job market and work-related technologies are necessitating continuous education. In some sectors, the potential exists for AI and other forms of automation to eliminate 50–80% of the work currently undertaken by professionals and skilled workers.
>
> *(Item #40)*

At this point we need to define what we mean by knowledge and knowledge management. What is knowledge and why is it important? Knowledge can be defined as what information, understanding or skill we gain from either experience or education. It is fundamentally an awareness of what is going on around us and our understanding of that situation. Knowledge has also been defined as the human faculty resulting from interpreted information; understanding that germinates from a combination of data, information, experience and individual interpretation. The Merriam-Webster dictionary defines knowledge as "the fact or condition of knowing something with familiarity gained through experience or association" and " the circumstance or condition of apprehending truth or fact through reasoning: cognition" (Merriam-Webster.com, undated).

Knowledge management, on the other hand, are those strategies and processes designed to identify, capture, structure, value, leverage and share an organization's (or individual's) intellectual assets to enhance performance and competitiveness. It is based on two critical activities: (1) the capture and documentation of individual explicit and tacit knowledge, and (2) its dissemination within the organization (BusinessDictionary.com). Knowledge management has also been defined by Gupta and McDaniel (2002) as "the creative mining of information from diverse sources with the purpose of business opportunities in mind. As a firm works diligently toward perusing its information assets through the multitude of perceptual filters available, high-impact, matchless gems are unearthed, which have the potential to substantially affect the bottom-line" (p. 41). They make a useful distinction between knowledge management and information management noting that "the former implies a persistent, intentional effort of extracting from available information what is critical for business success, while the latter is more concerned with making critical information available in a timely and consistent manner to end-users within the organizational structure" (p. 41). Therefore, knowledge management is the deliberate and purposeful process of capturing valuable knowledge (intellectual capital) of people throughout the organization, making that knowledge available to people who need it (knowledge sharing/transfer), and then using that knowledge to create new knowledge (innovation) or use the knowledge to solve problems or make better decisions.

It is useful at this point to clarify the meaning of innovation and its links with knowledge management. According to Harkema and Browaeys (2002)

> innovation refers to an invention, which can either be a new product or service. Innovation processes refer to the stages an invention has to go through before it is launched in the market (e.g. Utterback, 1994). Sources of innovation can either be incremental technological advancements or radical breakthroughs, or customer needs, preferences and wishes.

Parlby and Taylor (2000) are of the opinion that knowledge management is about supporting innovation, the generation of new ideas and the exploitation of the organization's thinking power. Cavusgil et al. (2003) argue that knowledge management is a mechanism through which innovation complexity can be addressed. Knowledge management can manage new knowledge through the innovation process, as well as managing existing knowledge as a resource used as input to the innovation process. Perhaps the best way to understand the link between innovation and knowledge management is to recognize that innovation is a process that opens the opportunity for knowledge to be combined and recombined in new not previously thought ways (Du Plessis, 2007). This clearly links the need for knowledge management, knowledge transfer and innovation in organizations of the future. We would argue that skills in these three arenas are crucial for survival for every organization, large and small. A practical aspect of knowledge is what some term "knowledge sharing". Knowledge sharing is the activity by which knowledge is exchanged among people and organizations. Knowledge sharing can be seen from the view of an individual seeking out knowledge (knowledge pull if you will) or when knowledge is "pushed" to members of the organization via various communication tools.

But let's step back from definitions and look at a few famous examples throughout history that remind us of the huge value of knowledge. Military stories are especially important here because the stakes are so high, often involving life and death situations.

Example #1: British and French Battles over 100 Years

This example is drawn from (Luecke, 1993).

At the battle of Crecy (1346) the English used the longbow for the first time. This yielded a strategic and tactical advantage over the French as the longbow could send an arrow much further than existing bows of the time and could be reloaded much faster (a well-trained bowman could fire 10 arrows a minute).

4 Knowledge? What Knowledge?

The British, under the leadership of King Edward III numbered approximately 12,000 (of which 7,000 were bowman) and faced 36,000 French soldiers (depending on the sources it could have been a bit larger or a bit smaller). The French made 14–16 charges against the British lines and the British archers fired approximately 500,000 arrows. The French suffered enormous losses (the numbers range from 12,000–30,000 depending on the source) and it was a stunning victory for the much smaller British Army from the use of "new" technology.

Note that in this particular example, the French were exposed to knowledge they did not have in the form of a long bow. They now knew what they did not know in Figure 1.1 above. But did they actually acquire this knowledge and use it?

Nearly 70 years later in 1415 at the battle of Agincourt, once again, a numerically smaller British Army (7,000 bowman and 1,500 other soldiers) was led by King Henry V. The English were outnumbered by 4:1. The results were exactly as with Crecy. The lowest estimate of French dead is 4,000 (with a high estimate of 11,000), while the British lost less than 150. The decisive factor in the English victory was, again, the use of the longbow.

It is unclear why the French did not apparently use the knowledge gained in 1346 from the lessons of Crecy and transfer that knowledge *before* the battle of Agincourt.

Our point is simple, but we believe powerful—knowledge that is "discovered" but not shared or transferred is not acted upon, and if not acted upon or transferred the result can be disastrous. In addition, knowledge that is not realized can inhibit future innovations. But let us turn our attention to a more modern example of knowledge management failures.

Example #2: Lessons Not Learned from World War I to World War II

In the 1930s after many of France's young men had been killed in WWI, France built a strong fortification that they called the "Maginot Line" (see strong fortification; solid line in Figure 1.2). This was a line of concrete fortifications, tank obstacles, artillery casemates, machine gun posts and other defenses. The commanders believed that the knowledge they had gained from the Word War I would be important to use in the pending second war with Germany.

These fortifications stretched from the Swiss border to the Ardennes Forest. The British and French thought that these Maginot fortifications would prevent the Germans from attacking through this line. Therefore, they moved the majority of their soldiers and equipment to the border of Luxemburg and Belgium (see weak fortifications; dotted line in Figure 1.2).

They assumed that the Germans would invade France through the Low Countries (Belgium and Luxembourg) as they had in 1914. However, the British and French could not move their troops into the Low Countries (Belgium and Holland) at that time because those countries were neutral. However, they planned that once the Germans attacked the Low Countries, the Allies would swing their armies like a gate through the Low Countries to prevent the Germans from entering France. The pivot point of this gate was the Ardennes forest at the northern tip of the Maginot line. The French assumed this forested area to be essentially impassable with modern heavy equipment and therefore, it was poorly protected. In May of 1940, just as the French expected, the Germans entered the Low Countries mirroring the Schlieffen plan of 1914 and the British and French swung their armies like a gate through Belgium to stop the German advance. Once the British and French did this, the German Army group entered the Ardennes forest, preceded by highly trained engineering battalions that cleared the way and promptly outflanked the Allied forces, making the Maginot line useless and trapping a large portion of the French Army and nearly all of the British expeditionary force between two Army groups and the sea (http://en.wikipedia.org/wiki/Battle_of_France). One source claimed that there were almost 2.3 million casualties with about 380,000 Allied Soldiers killed (http://5bloodiestbattlesofwwii.weebly.com/battle-of-france.html).

The Allied leaders used old knowledge and made assumptions based on this that proved to be fatal. What is interesting is that the German leaders similarly studied old knowledge, old strategies, and then, searched for new, innovative knowledge to give them a competitive advantage. In other words, the German leaders acted on "newly" developed knowledge and innovation. In this case, it was developing new ways to get equipment and troops through the Ardennes forest which the Allies believed to be impassable. We can infer that the culture of the Allied leaders created a type of "groupthink" mentality that led to their not testing "what they knew" to be true and therefore acting on incorrect or corrupt knowledge.

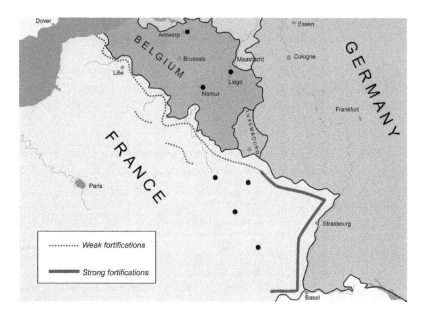

FIGURE 1.2 The Maginot Line

6 Knowledge? What Knowledge?

Fast forward to the winter of 1944. The Allies had just liberated much of France and were stretched thin because of their quick advance through the area. The Germans were in retreat and had suffered heavy casualties and were running out of fuel. Because it was winter, the roads were mud and ice, so the Allies assumed that the Germans were in no position to attack. The Allies had advanced quickly through France, and because of the bad weather conditions, the planes also had a hard time with aerial reconnaissance. The Germans massed a large striking force near the Ardennes and similar to what they did in 1940, moved through the Ardennes and attacked the American lines. The attack was completely unexpected. Advance German units in Allied uniforms that spoke English had moved through the lines before the attack to take control of important intersections, preserve road signs, misdirect Allied troops and attempt to secure fuel supplies from the Allies. When the attack came, the Allies were unprepared, surprised and confused by the subversive German efforts—that is, the Allies did not absorb the knowledge obtained in 1940 in their planning and were caught off guard. The German force was able to create a large bulge in the Allied line before the advance eventually petered out and they were defeated, but with about 186,000 casualties (http://en.wikipedia.org/wiki/Battle_of_the_Bulge).

Amazingly, the Germans did essentially the same thing twice. The Allies did not learn from their prior experience just 4 years earlier and suffered from a lack of intelligence in both situations. They also suffered from a lack of innovative thinking because the Allied commanders in both situations underestimated the Germans, used bad or at best incomplete knowledge and bad assumptions.

What can businesses learn from this and why should we care? Well, let's start by looking at an iconic U.S. company that did not value knowledge creation or knowledge transfer.

This story comes from the *New York Times* (Solomon, 2014).

> The story of RadioShack begins with failure. The company, founded in 1921, sold radio parts and surplus supplies by outlet and catalog. But it was almost bankrupt when it was purchased in 1963 by Tandy Corporation, a leather retailer.

At the time, RadioShack had just nine stores. But it expanded rapidly to become a hobbyist's dream. RadioShack became a mythical place for all things related to electronics, catering not just to the do-it-yourselfers but to anyone in search of the latest gadgets.

Fast forward to 2015, when RadioShack underwent bankruptcy. According to ABC news,

> It's a sad day for tinkerers. America could be about to say goodbye to RadioShack. All its stores may close in the near future. Bloomberg reports RadioShack "is preparing to shut down the almost-century-old retail chain

in a bankruptcy deal that would sell about half its store leases to Sprint and close the rest", according to sources. The New York Stock Exchange plans to delist RadioShack shares.

(Davies, 2015)

What happened? The *New York Times* article suggested that "RadioShack suffered from poor, often overpaid, leadership, which could not focus on a single plan and then was left grasping for a rescue strategy."

It was interesting to search through online blogs about the corporate culture at RadioShack. We observed comments like "The morale is really low at the stores and district managers are really lame, nothing but cheerleaders that don't understand what's going on and what would really sell and they don't want to hear it." Another former employee described RadioShack as having a "broken business model and dysfunctional management".

A story in Forbes further examined the lack of knowledge and dysfunctional culture at RadioShack: Their core was not just people who love tech, but people who made tech. With the rise of hardcore technophiles over the last 20 years, the Shack [sic] could have played a major role. They could have made a play in helping STEM (science, technology, engineering and math) education in schools. While everyone else took those miscellaneous parts and made something of themselves (remember that at the core of every smartphone is a very smart radio), RadioShack remained a miscellany of lost opportunity. Instead of becoming a beacon for those aspiring to Silicon Valley mansions, they stayed a Shack.

(Hanlon, 2015)

Like the Allied Forces in 1940 and the French over an 80-year period in two separate battles, the people at RadioShack did not appear to seek valuable knowledge and thus, did not know their "enemy" (their competitors) or their customers, leading to decline and ultimate "death" (bankruptcy). Another commonality appears to be a culture of "we know it all" so that "we do not have to seek new knowledge". Apparently, many U.S. businesses may not recognize the value of knowledge based on some recent data.

The U.S. used to have the most competitive business climate and the most innovative business culture in the world, leading to a high standard of living. However, today U.S. jobs are going overseas. There is an unacceptable lower standard of living for many "main street" people in this country. Many businesses are failing or struggling to survive. If you adjust average wages for an "apples to apples" comparison, the average worker in the U.S. made about $7.50 per hour from about 1900 to 1935. The average wage peaked at about $20/hour in 1975. By 2015, it was down to about $8.50/hour, representing a 57% decrease in that 40-year period (Nielson, 2012).

8 Knowledge? What Knowledge?

We know that poor knowledge leads to disasters and decline. On the other hand, can we provide an example of a company that recognizes the value of knowledge creation and knowledge transfer for competitive advantage—that is, a success story using knowledge? We will call this story: "Innovation drives economic growth."

Forbes Magazine has ranked Salesforce.com the most innovative company in the world for at least 4 years in a row. This software company that develops customer relationship management systems showed a 35.6% sales growth in 2014 with a 24% 5-year total annualized total return. How did they achieve this? They are always scanning the environment for new knowledge, new trends, and they have learned to harness this knowledge for innovation in their products, services and meeting customer needs (www.forbes.com/innovative-companies/). In addition, they use practices found to be effective in the military such as "boot camp" for intensive training and socialization including developing strong relationships and trust among people across the world. They also use their knowledge and technologies effectively.

> It gathers, organizes, and disseminates everything there is to know about which products are selling, which customers are buying, and how the sales staff is performing; it integrates with Facebook, Twitter, etc.; it deploys as needed to desktops, laptops, tablets, and smartphones from its home in the cloud.
>
> *(Whitford, 2014)*

That was a knowledge success story in business, and reflects a continuing focus on moving from what "we do not know" to "what we know". Here is a more individual example of knowledge management in action from an Army Ranger Captain in the urban battlefield of Iraq:

It was during the intense time in Iraq; about 2005. Captain Bob (name disguised), an experienced Army Ranger, was setting up a watch point in the city. Based on his concentrated study of battles in Iraq, intense training in urban combat and tactical maneuvers as well as two prior tours of duty in Iraq, he was able to quickly scan the environment: streets, escape routes, visibility from different positions, buildings, cars and other things like cement barriers. He had learned to think like the enemy. Where would they likely position themselves, where would their escape routes be, what kind of firepower would they use? All this accumulated "tacit" knowledge allowed him to determine a good vantage point to set up his unit for the night. It did not take long for the first shots to arrive from the enemy. However, due to his knowledge, his Soldiers had good cover, a good vantage point to return fire to take out the enemy and prevent their easy escape. Thus, he was able to use his knowledge that he had learned in previous deployments effectively for good reconnaissance, the ability to outwit the enemy and keep his soldiers safe.

The moral of this story is that this Army Ranger trained relentlessly, relied on "muscle memory", accumulated knowledge and the ability to communicate and share crucial information under stressful conditions to use valuable knowledge effectively to ultimately take out the enemy and survive.

Explicit and Tacit Knowledge

We noted "tacit" knowledge above and we need to explain what we mean. There are two generally accepted and acknowledged types of knowledge: explicit and tacit knowledge, both are important, and neither is complete without the other. Explicit knowledge is the easiest to describe and understand. It is knowledge that can be spoken, communicated, transmitted, processed and stored relatively easily. It is information that is interpreted, put in context and anchored in beliefs and commitments of individuals (Nonaka et al., 2000) and as such, subject to easy codification, storage and retrieval. This is the type of "knowledge" that most individuals, firms and organizations are familiar with, and can be found in the codification of plans, reports, operating manuals, scientific formulas and patents (Seidler-de Alwis and Hartmann, 2008). Generally speaking, explicit knowledge is the process and product by which knowledge is communicated throughout the organization—it is akin to the shift from knowing what you do not know—to knowing and communicating that to others. As such, it is a reflection of what the organization (or individual) has learned in the past and has codified—it is not the "newest" knowledge.

Although explicit knowledge is important to the operation of any organization—it is tacit knowledge that is crucial to survival and long-term success. Tacit knowledge is far more difficult to describe and explain—it is reflected in the procedures, rooted in action and is acquired by the sharing of experiences, by observation and by imitation. The after-action reviews (AARs) done in the military are an example of tacit knowledge transfer. After a mission, the troops will gather together and share what they experienced and what they learned so that everyone in the team can learn from this collective knowledge and improve everyone's performance on the next mission. Tacit knowledge yields insights necessary for the understanding of explicit knowledge and for the placement of that knowledge in context. According to Kikoski and Kikoski (2004) it is tacit knowledge that creates the learning curve for others to follow and ultimately provides the competitive advantage for long-term success. Ideally, an organization will capture valuable tacit knowledge and convert it into explicit knowledge so that it can be effectively shared. For example, in Iraq, Army Ranger Captain Bob would have gathered his team together after the battle that we described and gathered the information and knowledge that everyone experienced minutes earlier. He (or an intelligence officer) would have recorded that knowledge to look for new, valuable lessons learned in enemy strategies, IEDs, etc. so that it could be codified into explicit knowledge and shared with other units in country or about to deploy. Our Ranger Captain might not realize it, but the process by which he obtained knowledge, codified it and shared and transferred it is captured in Figure 1.3 below. What is important to recognize here is that knowledge acquisition, sharing and transferring is an ongoing continuous process for both individuals and organizations. How does this relate to knowledge management? It is well documented that knowledge represents perhaps the most crucial asset within any organization. It serves as the source of continual innovation via new ideas, process improvement

10 Knowledge? What Knowledge?

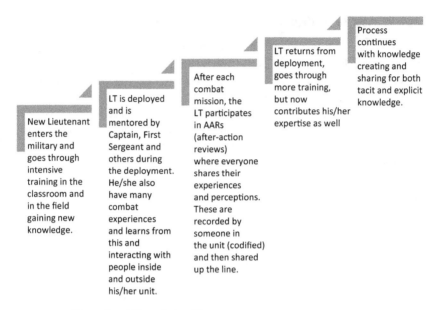

FIGURE 1.3 Example of Knowledge Flow

and arguably the true source of sustainable competitive advantage. Thus, the ability to effectively harness knowledge as well as create new knowledge and share it within an organization essentially constitutes the field of knowledge management.

While there is no "silver bullet" in this field, knowledge management has been studied for many years in the areas of knowledge creation, knowledge transfer, and knowledge storage and access (see, for example Chen et al., 2011; Zheng et al., 2010). It is well documented that explicit knowledge, which is codified into reports or processes like software programs represents the easy part of knowledge management. This codified knowledge can be easily stored in databases, easily queried and transferred across the building or across the globe via the Internet or intranets. Knowledge bases that are well managed, filtered for relevancy and recency and monitored by subject matter experts have been found effective for knowledge transfer across organizations. Knowledge maps showing where crucial expertise is located within an organization is similarly useful and relatively easy to administer (Wang and Belardo, 2005).

Tacit knowledge, on the other hand, remains more elusive. This type of knowledge resides within the individual in "the little grey cells" (Christie, 1959) and results from cumulative experiences, learning and reflection. It is difficult to codify and transfer for many reasons (Nonaka et al., 2000; Seidler-de Alwis and Hartmann, 2008; Kikoski and Kikoski, 2004). Many people have vast knowledge in different areas, but do not know how to articulate and communicate it. They may not know that their knowledge is important or relevant in different situations, or may not even be aware of the depth of their knowledge. People may also not want to share their knowledge if it represents a source of power or job security.

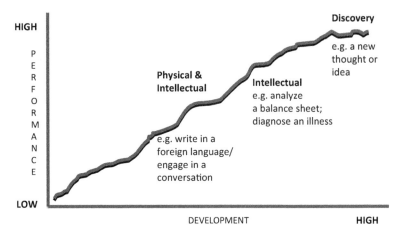

FIGURE 1.4 The Relationship of Tacit Knowledge Development and Performance (Kikoski and Kikoski, 2004)

How organizations develop, store and transfer knowledge is becoming increasingly important. Yet, organizations seem to struggle with obtaining knowledge, maintaining that knowledge over time and transferring it throughout the organization so that all elements could benefit. In Figure 1.4 we address the relationship between tacit knowledge development and performance over time.

A Conceptual Map of this Book

A visual portrayal of how this book will unfold is shown in Figure 1.5 below. In the next chapter we will address explosive innovation and how organizations can put knowledge to work. The following two chapters will address the powerful influences of leadership and culture on the process of knowledge management. We then turn our attention to a little discussed or analyzed aspect of knowledge management—that of knowledge corruption and knowledge hoarding. We then look more closely at the role of training and socialization in the management of knowledge and follow that with a closer look at knowledge structure and processes in organizations. No discussion of knowledge management would be complete without recognizing the subtle and pervasive impact of technologies and social media on all aspects of knowledge. We conclude this work by putting this all together with insights and suggestions for improved knowledgemanagement in organizations. We are *not interested* in exploring in detail leadership or culture or any of the topics herein related to knowledge—there is an enormous literature that addresses these in detail. We are interested in the relationship of those areas to the use, acquisition, transfer and management of knowledge and innovation. We will also provide some checklists and approaches to assessing the state of knowledge management in your organization.

12 Knowledge? What Knowledge?

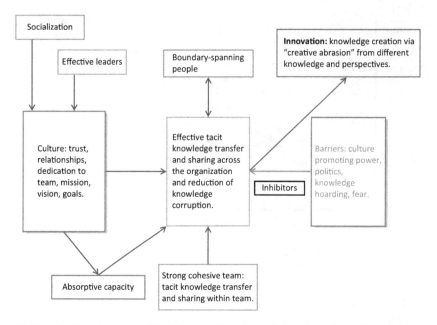

FIGURE 1.5 Relationships of Variables in Tacit Knowledge Transfer and Potential Knowledge Corruption

Knowledge Management in Practice

At the end of each chapter we conclude with two sets of observations that we believe you will find useful. The first is a set of concise lessons and/or questions that you can take back to your organization or consider with regards to your personal knowledge practice. The second is what we are terming "Veteran Observations" on knowledge management drawn from our interviews with Veterans.

1. Do you know "what you do not know you know?" How can you move your knowledge here to "knowing what you know?"
2. What "tacit" knowledge do you have that is not explicit? How would a person succeeding you become aware of this knowledge?
3. When you interact with your colleagues, do you get the sense that they possess tacit knowledge you do not have? How might you explore that and begin to share this knowledge across the organization?
4. How often do you challenge "conventional thinking" and revisit the assumptions from the perspective of developing new knowledge?

References

Cavusgil, S., Calantone, R. and Zhao, Y. (2003). "Tacit knowledge transfer and firm innovation capability." *The Journal of Business & Industrial Marketing*, Vol. 18 No. 1: 6–21.

Chen, P., Pollard, D. and Puriveth, P. (2011). "Implementing knowledge management." *Journal of Business and Economics Research*, Vol. 2 No. 5: 7–15.

Christie, A. (1959). *Murder on the Orient Express*. Pioneer Drama Service, Inc.

Davies, R. (2015). "RadioShack Reportedly 'Preparing to Shut Down'", available at http://abcnews.go.com/blogs/business/2015/02/radio-shack-reportedly-preparing-to-shut-down/ (accessed March, 2016).

Du Plessis, M. (2007). "The role of knowledge management in innovation." *Journal of Knowledge Management*, Vol. 11 No. 4: 20–29.

Gupta, A. and McDaniel, J. (2002). "Creating competitive advantage by effectively managing knowledge: A framework for knowledge management." *Journal of Knowledge Management Practice*, Vol. 3 No. 2: 40–49.

Hanlon, P. (2015). "RadioShack Demise Sends Beacon for Beacon Brands", available at www.forbes.com/sites/patrickhanlon/2015/02/10/radio-shack-demise-sends-beacon-for-beacon-brands/2/ (accessed March, 2016).

Harkema, S. J. M. and Browaeys, M. J. (2002). "Managing innovation successfully: A complex process." *Journal of International Development*, Vol. 17: 611–630. In European Academy of Management Annual Conference Proceedings, EURAM.

Kikoski, C. K. and Kikoski, J. F. (2004). *The Inquiring Organization: Tacit Knowledge, Conversation, and Knowledge Creation Skills for 21st-Century Organizations*. Westport, CT and London: Praeger.

Luecke, R. A. (1993). *Scuttle Your Ships Before Advancing: And Other Lessons from History on Leadership and Change for Todays Managers*. New York: Oxford University Press.

Meriam-Webster.com. (N.D.). "Knowledge", available at www.merriam-webster.com/dictionary/knowledge (accessed January, 2018).

Nielson, J. (2012). "U.S. Standard of Living Has Fallen More Than 50%: Opinion", available at www.thestreet.com/story/11480568/1/us-standard-of-living-has-fallen-more-than-50-opinion.html (accessed March, 2016).

Nonaka, I., Toyama, R. and Konno, N. (2000). "SECI, BA and leadership: A unified model of dynamic knowledge creation." *Long Range Planning*, Vol. 33: 4–34.

Parlby, D. and Taylor, R. (2000). "The Power of Knowledge: A Business Guide to Knowledge Management", available at: www.kpmgconsulting.com/index.html (accessed December, 2016).

Seidler-de Alwis, R. and Hartmann, E. (2008). "The use of tacit knowledge within innovative research." *Journal of Knowledge Management*, Vol. 63 No. 7: 763–771.

Solomon, S. (2014). "A History of Misses for RadioShack", Dealbook, NY Times, available at https://dealbook.nytimes.com/2014/09/16/for-radioshack-a-history-of-misses/?_r=0 (accessed March 3, 2016).

Talwar, R. and Lazarova, I. (N.D.). "Driving Forces – 100 Trends and Developments Shaping the Path to 2025," available at http://thefuturesagency.com/wp-content/uploads/2013/04/Driving-Forces-100-Trends-and-Developments-Shaping-the-Path-to-2025-Master.pdf (accessed February 1, 2017).

Utterback, J. M. (1994). *Mastering the Dynamics of Innovation*. Boston: Harvard Business School Press.

Wang, W. and Belardo, S. (2005). "Strategic Integration: A Knowledge Management Approach to Crisis Management", published in: *System Sciences, 2005*. HICSS '05. Proceedings of the 38th Annual Hawaii International Conference.

Whitford, D. (2014). "Salesforce.com: The Software and the Story", Inc.com, available at www.inc.com/magazine/201409/david-whitford/inc.500-sales-force-boot-camp-produces-modern-salesman.html (accessed March, 2016).

Zheng, W., Yang, B. and McLean, G. N. (2010). "Linking organizational culture, structure, strategy, and organizational effectiveness: Mediating role of knowledge management." *Journal of Business Research*, Vol. 63 No. 7: 763–771.

2

EXPLOSIVE INNOVATION
Putting Knowledge to Work

> The greatest enemy of knowledge is not ignorance, it is the illusion of knowledge.
> —*Stephen Hawking*

In Chapter 1, we set the foundation for *why* effective knowledge transfer represents the most critical cause for the success or failure of an organization; whether it is in business, the military or non-profit. In this chapter, we go into more detail on just how serious this is and provide concrete strategies to improve knowledge transfer, innovation and performance. We discuss the value of "good" knowledge; that which is valuable and effectively used to improve something in the organization verses "bad" knowledge, such as someone's knowledge that is obsolete, simply incorrect, or not valid in some way, which often leads to bad decisions and negative results. The concept of innovation is then explored as a source of sustainable competitive advantage resulting from good knowledge sharing and knowledge creation. We reiterate that we use the terms "knowledge transfer" and "knowledge sharing" interchangeably throughout the book.

Innovation

It is also important at this point to explain what we mean by "innovation" and why this is so critically important to the success and performance of an organization. A simple definition from "businessdictionary.com" is "The process of translating an idea or invention into a good or service that creates value or for which customers will pay." Another definition is "Innovation is significant positive change" (Berkun, 2013). There are many reasons why this is important

(Ikeda and Marshall, 2016). First, the world is a hyper competitive place. Organizations that do NOT innovate and instead remain complacent will be supplanted by those that improve products, reduce costs, better satisfy customer needs and the list goes on. Customer expectations are also very high where product and process life cycles continue to shrink as people seek new, better, more interesting solutions.

Let's take a look at Apple to see this in action (Elmansy, undated):

> When Steve Jobs returned to Apple after being fired, the company share was only worth U.S. $5 and its future was uncertain. In 2016, Apple's share price was around U.S. $108 and the company achieved revenues of U.S. $233.7 billion in 2015 with net income of U.S. $53.39 billion. This mini case study sheds light on the role that design thinking and innovation played in helping Steve Jobs rescue Apple with his consumer-driven strategy and vision for the company.

How did Apple successfully use innovation to achieve this?

When Steve Jobs was fired from Apple in 1985, the company was struggling as it tried to compete unsuccessfully with IBM and other giants. However, when he returned in 1997, he reintroduced an innovation-driven culture where associates focused on customer's needs and desires including simplicity, ease of use, and beautiful products that redefined the way people lived and worked. They use an approach called "network innovation" where they proactively seek knowledge and ideas from both in-house and outside sources and bring them together with a focus on innovation and customer needs to continually innovate. The results, as shown in the story box above, are clear.

However, let's back up and look at types of knowledge as they relate ultimately to innovation.

The Impact of Bad Knowledge

A leader's job is to make good strategic decisions for the business. However, this is easier said than done since we often "don't know what we don't know" and make (sometimes catastrophic) decisions with bad knowledge (Hetherington, 2008).

It is fascinating to read Daniel J. Power's article about the consequences of bad decisions. He provides research from Gary Cokins' (2015) work which showed that "almost half of the roughly 25 companies that passed the rigorous tests to be listed in the once-famous book by Tom Peters and Robert Waterman, *In Search of Excellence* (1989), today either no longer exist, are in bankruptcy, or have

16 Explosive Innovation

performed poorly." Also, of the companies on the original Standard and Poor's (S&P) 500 Index created in 1957 only 74 or just 15 percent remain on the list in 2014 (Peters, 1989; Cokins, 2015; Power, 2016).

Let's look at one of America's most iconic companies—Sears. "Sears reflected everyday Americans' way of life" (Sweeney, 2012). By 2016, Sears, the once mighty face of the U.S. economic success story, was struggling to survive. Today, it continues to close stores and is facing possible bankruptcy. Why? What decisions were made or not made that led to this disastrous decline? According to Brigid Sweeney (2012), Sears originally anticipated changes in the marketplace and responded to them, in essence, Sears was able to read the changes in its competitive environment, gain knowledge from those changes and more importantly act upon them. The leaders made decisions based on this never-ending knowledge acquisition process such as the appeal of "mail-order when America was young and rural". Then, correctly foreseeing the rise of the automobile and the shift to cities, it began building stores located in the center of cities to be easily accessible to its evolving customer base. As people fled the cities for the suburbs, Sears followed and was a major player in the suburban shopping mall revolution of the 1960s: Sears seemingly anchored every last one and was a fine example of knowledge management in action, taking steps to innovate in its delivery of goods and services and in physical location to anticipate the changes in its customer's preferences.

However, by the beginning of the 21st century, this changed. There was an old saying that the decline of imperial China happened with an Emperor who declared that "anything worth knowing resided in China". This attitude of complacency meant that no new ideas from outside the inner circle were ever considered, leading to an eventual "death spiral where innovation using knowledge was no longer a norm". The same thing happened to Sears. The leaders of the organization stopped searching for emerging trends and changes in the marketplace and made decisions based on what had worked before. We believe that this happens often in *very successful* organizations over time. How did this happen to the once mighty Sears? According to one story, Sears

> executives spent too much time investing in side businesses and ignored the competition. This did not have to be fatal; however, it actually starved those resources (capital and management) from the retail business, leaving it unable to respond and adapt to the needs of the evolving consumer and marketplace.
>
> *(Lutz, 2015)*

Another example of bad decisions and bad knowledge comes from Eastman Kodak. They actually developed the first digital camera in 1975, but had the illusion of knowledge dominance in the areas of technologies and consumer trends. Therefore, they refused to listen to their engineers who warned them about the threat of digital photography and the use of the core technology of the cell phone for taking photos. As we all know, this illusion of knowledge about their products and future markets was the basis for their attitudes of denial and complacency that led to their "death spiral". The result was that they filed for bankruptcy in 2012. In other words, the leaders did not know what they did not know and refused to listen to people who attempted to tell them. This is the ultimate challenge to developing knowledge management—complacency and the belief that what is now "known" is all that is needed for success.

A recent example of bad knowledge from one of our Veterans happened during the early days in the invasion of Iraq:

> In his second tour of duty in Iraq, the infantry wanted to put concrete blast walls all over the place. Our Sergeant had knowledge about the limitations of his armored vehicles and advised the infantry guys that the vehicles did not have the power to push these concrete barriers. However, our Sergeant's advice was ignored and he was ordered to use the tanks and other armored vehicles to push the concrete blast walls into place. While this served a purpose of providing a shield for the infantry, it also caused the transmissions of the vehicles to break down, so that they were "dead in the water" when needed desperately in combat.

Why is it that bad knowledge and bad attitudes lead to disaster? Mark Twain once said, "The trouble with the world is not that people know too little, but that they know so many things that ain't so."

The moral of this story is that the first prerequisite to using knowledge effectively for good decisions, innovation and success lies in the ability of people to develop a humbleness in recognizing that they often do not know what they do not know and continually learn and seek new knowledge. Again, attitudes and culture influence leader's willingness to learn and seek new knowledge (e.g. they know that they do not know important knowledge and are willing and open to learning). This is in contrast to leaders who are more complacent and perhaps even arrogant about their level of knowledge and do not care that they "do not know what they do not know".

The Power of Good Knowledge

Peter Drucker once observed that the best way to predict the future is to create it. Others have noted that knowledge becomes power only when we put it into use—which is a major theme of this book and is reflected in our Army Ranger's experience as show in texted box.

18 Explosive Innovation

PUTTING KNOWLEDGE TO USE

Here is a story from our Army Ranger Captain? Veteran (Iraq War): One of his Sergeants was able to detect IEDs really well based on his great amount of experience in the field (accumulated knowledge). The enemy would put a bomb inside a curbstone or other common things and the SGT was therefore able to detect when something on the road did not look right. For example, he noticed a muffler on the side of the road that was too clean and did not look right. This SGT had developed an "intuition" that allowed him to detect IEDs that most other people would not notice. Therefore, this Captain learned from his SGT and in later deployments, was similarly able to detect IEDs. He also had studied what artillery shells looked like as well as different IEDs and was able to detect them where others missed them. He probably saved the lives of tens or hundreds of his troops with this acquired knowledge and his never-ending thirst for continual learning and knowledge acquisition.

Let's take a look at a company that is known for continual learning and always seeking new knowledge—3M.

3M is known for innovation. Here are a few stories that demonstrate the power of collaboration and knowledge sharing to harness innovation for competitive advantage. When looking at this example, you will see that they use proactive collaboration, environmental scanning, new knowledge creation and knowledge sharing and transfer to achieve innovation, new market development and sustainable competitive advantage. This first example comes from 3M itself (Delaney, 2013).

The Tour de France, established in 1903, is an intense bicycle competition that puts the best cyclists in the world to the test. Someone at 3M noticed that technology provides competitors in the race competitive advantages in terms of the weight of the bicycles: the lighter and stiffer the bicycle, the better the performance for the racer. However, with existing technologies at that time, making a bicycle frame lighter meant sacrificing the stiffness, so riders had to choose between lightweight or stiff models.

When an observant engineer at 3M saw this dilemma, he also had knowledge of 3M's pioneering research in nano-engineering where they were working at reducing particle sizes to make new, innovative materials that were both lighter and stiffer than any existing materials. By establishing a culture of collaboration and communication, the engineer working on this project was able to collaborate with fellow engineers and also find a bicycle manufacturer who represented a good fit for collaboration: Cervélo. Because Cervélo also had a culture that embraced innovation and collaboration, they were able to understand the value of this new material as 3M shared that knowledge with them and they used it to produce bicycles that were superior to any on the market and offered both stiff-ness and light weight.

People with knowledge of this new field of nano-technology were also able to develop a vision for uses in other industries, such as aerospace to make airplanes stronger and lighter among others. In other words, they were able to take this "new knowledge" into new fields of endeavor.

Why Is This Important?

The point is that 3M had developed over time a culture of knowledge sharing, continual learning, collaboration and communication that created innovation, a sustainable competitive advantage and business success. With about 85,000 employees spread over 60 countries, this is no easy task.

How Did They Do This?

They accomplish this with a sincere devotion to encouraging risk-taking, idea-generation and ways to generate and share knowledge across the organization.

- They have developed forums across the globe where employees can share knowledge, generate new ideas and work collaboratively.
- They hold knowledge conferences that bring people from different areas of expertise and different geographic areas together to share knowledge and generate new ideas.
- They communicate proactively with customers and develop long term rela-tionships to understand the meet customer's evolving needs.
- Finally, they build metrics into knowledge creation and sharing and reward people for collaboration, knowledge sharing and resulting innovation.

Can your company do this? As we will discuss in Chapters 3 (leadership) and 4 (culture), it will depend on whether you have leaders who can develop and promote a shared vision and mission for something that everyone buys into. It will also involve a cultural shift to the qualities and values mentioned: continual thirst for knowledge and learning, trust and respect for colleagues with a desire to share knowledge and collaborate among other criteria.

How Does the Military Use Knowledge Effectively?

In Chapter 1, we shared stories about the impact of bad knowledge in different military battles including the annihilation of the French forces twice at Crecy and Agincourt as well as the huge number of casualties in the Ardennes forest during World War II (Battle of the Bulge). We have seen that bad knowledge can lead to catastrophic consequences on the battlefield.

20 Explosive Innovation

Given this urgency for good knowledge, how does the military leverage knowledge effectively to try to bring everyone home alive and well?

As we will discuss in the chapters on culture and leadership, the military has recognized the crucial role that values and attitudes play in this game in terms of the need for good quality knowledge and continual learning.

In a recent report by the United States Strategic Command (Thon and Steinhauser, 2009), they stated that:

> The post-9/11 threat environment is characterized as complex and unstable. DoD organizations must be able to respond through creativity, innovation, and flexibility . . . [with] the need to increase knowledge sharing, mutual understanding, and collaborative decision-making. Leveraging our human resources is critical to creating a learning organization that facilitates knowledge transfer.
>
> *(p. 4)*

The U.S. military recognizes that effective and efficient knowledge transfer is crucial to support national security in a post-9/11 turbulent environment.

The military is also smart in understanding that the enemy also continually develops and adapts knowledge-intensive strategies and attitudes in response to our improvements in these same areas.

An interesting story about the power of knowledge came from our World War II Veteran during the Battle of the Bulge where there were about 75,000 American casualties (U.S. Army Center of Military History, 2011):

> Because ammunition was in short supply, he taught his men how to listen for the sound and pattern of firing their guns during a battle so that they could fire in a controlled sequence to use the scarce ammunition as effectively as possible rather than wasting ammunition in chaotic "free for all" shooting.

Another thing he taught his troops was how to survive the brutal snow and ice.

> As the battle raged, blizzards and freezing rain often reduced visibility to almost zero. Frost covered much of the soldiers' equipment, and tanks had to be chiseled out of ice after they froze to the ground overnight. Many wounded soldiers froze to death before they were rescued, and thousands of American G.I.s were eventually treated for cases of frostbite and trench foot.
>
> *(Andrews, 2014)*

In our interview with the World War II Veteran who fought in the battle of the Bulge in the Ardennes, he said,

> Another example from the Battle of the Bulge, the Ardennes, was how to keep your feet dry. You had to share these secrets with your buddies or your feet would freeze, get frostbite or gangrene; have to be amputated. You had to change your socks every few hours. You would take the wet socks and keep 4-5 pairs wrapped around your waist to dry them. There were certain things like that that you had to train the replacements.

Many people wonder how ISIS (Islamic State) became so successful in gaining territory in the Middle East so quickly. A *New York Times* article (Hubbard and Schmitt, 2014) that explored this question came to these conclusions about the value of knowledge. The self-declared leader of ISIS, Abu Bakr al-Baghdadi, hand-picked his leadership team from among the men he met while a prisoner in American custody at the Camp Bucca detention center a decade ago. Many of his top leaders come from Saddam Hussein's former elite guard and the Baath Party. According to this article,

> The pedigree of its leadership, outlined by an Iraqi who has seen documents seized by the Iraqi military, as well as by American intelligence officials, helps explain its battlefield successes: Its leaders augmented traditional military skill with terrorist techniques refined through years of fighting American troops, while also having deep local knowledge and contacts. ISIS is in effect a hybrid of terrorists and an army.

What Can You Take Away From This to Help You or Your Organization?

While we know that there is no such thing as a "silver bullet", there are a few "golden nuggets" that we can take with us. From these business and military stories, the nuggets include:

- Develop, promote and nurture an attitude of humbleness throughout the organization where people recognize that they often "do not know what they do not know". Promote a perpetual quest for new knowledge, knowledge transfer, and using the knowledge to strive for innovation.
- Create a culture (addressed more deeply in Chapter 4) where people proactively seek and collaborate with others who have valuable knowledge.
- Create processes and structures (addressed more deeply in Chapter 7) and technologies (addressed more deeply in Chapter 8) that facilitate this.

22 Explosive Innovation

Finally, to explore the impact of good and bad knowledge on innovation, we suggest that there are several types of innovation that an organization can pursue through its knowledge strategies.

Types of Innovation

1. Product Innovation: For example, the stories about 3M and Apple earlier in this chapter showed the power of continual product innovation.
2. Process Innovation: A good example of process innovation would be Amazon.com where they continually seek new, better ways to improve the customer experience and deliver the product. For example, they pioneered the technology that "if you like this product, you might also like those". They also continually innovate to reduce costs and improve efficiencies and productivity. For example, Amazon pioneered the "one click" ordering that allowed customers to place their orders with simply clicking one button, avoiding the time-consuming entry of customer information, credit card information, etc.
3. Political–social Innovation: With the "Brexit" vote in the United Kingdom, which resulted in a decision to leave the EU, it has led, and will probably continue to lead, to new innovations from the political and social changes. For example, the financial sector will find new, innovative ways to efficiently transfer funds across European nations. Without the trading treaties, UK firms will innovate to find new ways to efficiently continue trading with European supply chain partners.
4. Geographic Innovation: This is shown in the Sears example above where they moved the physical location of their stores to adapt to customer migration. This is also seen in Walmart's evolution as a retail giant. Instead of challenging the largest retailers in the beginning of their existence, Walmart chose to go to smaller cities. Competitors laughed at them, noting that a large box store could not make money in those locations. The competitors were wrong, and Walmart's geographic innovation served as the basis for their eventual retail dominance.
5. A combination of any of the above

Lessons from Veterans

What is the impact of knowledge—good or bad? Some of the intense combat experiences from the Battle of the Bulge through Afghanistan shared common themes as noted below:

- All of these combat Veterans discovered that they needed to proactively and continually learn; seek out new knowledge so that they could understand the situation and make better decisions.

- The example from an Iraq War Veteran that exemplified this was a laser-sharp focus and vigilance to studying/learning about the environment around you.
- By developing an attitude that you must always be on your "A-game", always devote complete attention and energy to studying and learning about everyone around you, this will increase your chances of surviving the enemy attack and allow you to innovate and put knowledge to work immediately. One of the examples given was learning about anomalies in the environment. Since the enemy was always finding new ways to hide and attack, you had to devote intense study to everything around you. In this situation, the Captain spent many days and nights watching and studying the area, the streets and the people. He observed what appeared to be normal vs. atypical behaviors and eventually was able to learn and differentiate the normal civilians from the terrorists who looked the same on the surface. However, by learning about the atypical movements of the terrorists, he was able to anticipate their logistics and planned attacks and create his own defensive strategies to outmaneuver them and survive. Note that he was, in essence, paying acute attention to the evolving environment—a lesson that is sometimes lost on business executives
- This innovation and putting knowledge to work approach is reinforced by a Vietnam Veteran who described having a "vision" of what to expect when trying to rescue an Army unit that was surrounded by the Vietcong in an area that had dense vegetation. It made it extraordinarily difficult to see the Army unit and differentiate them from the Vietcong. However, the rescue operation that saved this unit of 20 Army infantry troops from a certain death was the result of intense training and field experiences in exactly this environment. He had flown countless missions in his Huey helicopter, learned the mentality and strategies of the Vietcong and also knew how his Army infantry troops would behave since he had formerly been an infantry officer before becoming a helicopter pilot. He never became complacent, never stopped studying and learning, and thus, developed an "intuition" or "vision" that allowed him to fly in, survey the densely vegetated area and develop a strategy to save his troops.
- One example of bad knowledge was from the Iraq War where an officer would NOT listen to the knowledge of our Veteran about using some tanks to move concrete walls. The officer's decision to not listen and learn from the knowledge and expertise of the Sargent was that the tanks were damaged, removing them from important combat missions, and possibly causing harm to troops in subsequent missions where those tanks were needed to combat the terrorists.

A Little Theory to Back the Propositions

For those of you who are not familiar with knowledge management, it is the ability of an organization to effectively harness and use the rare, non-imitable knowledge and expertise of its associates for sustainable competitive advantage.

24 Explosive Innovation

There are several widely accepted areas within knowledge management summarized here. First, there are two basic terms describing knowledge: "tacit knowledge"—that which is the accumulated knowledge from education, experiences, insights, observations, etc. It is ingrained in us and difficult to articulate, but is probably the most valuable form of knowledge since it frames our experiences, helps us with judgement and decisions. In contrast, "explicit knowledge" is that which can be codified; put into the words, sounds, or pictures that can be shared via written documents, videos, PowerPoint presentations, etc.

1. Knowledge acquisition: How does an organization acquire new, valuable knowledge? Some common methods include hiring people with needed knowledge and expertise, hiring outside consultants with the needed knowledge, or continual education and training of associated in the areas of knowledge and expertise needed for competitive advantage.

2. Knowledge generation/creation: How does an organization generate new, valuable knowledge? Some common methods include R&D (research and development) departments such as research labs within pharmaceutical companies. Another is the concept of "fusion"; bringing people with different expertise and perspectives together to come up with new and better answers to difficult problems, processes and projects. Dorothy Leonard-Barton (1995) coined the term "creative abrasion", which involves intentionally combining people with different skills, ideas and values to generate creative solutions. Similarly, creating networks and collaborations among people is often a successful strategy for new knowledge creation.

3. Knowledge codification: When you acquire or create new knowledge, it is helpful to codify it in some way so that it can be easily shared within or outside the organization. This involves Nonaka and Takeuchi's (1995) classic "knowledge spiral" (see Figure 2.1); a continuous cycle of four integrated processes:

    a. externalization (the process of articulating your unique "tacit" knowledge into something that can be understood by others; often in the form of stories, metaphors, etc.),

    b. combination (taking this new explicit knowledge, codifying it into documents, reports, videos, etc and sharing it),

    c. internalization (taking this new explicit knowledge from a report, video, etc. and learning from it; internalizing it into your own knowledge base)

    d. socialization (sharing your knowledge and experiences with others); usually via

    e. experiential interactions like mentoring, apprenticeships, etc.

4. Knowledge transfer: The next question is *how* to share both tacit and explicit knowledge effectively within and outside an organization? Sharing explicit knowledge is relatively easy. You can store and access documents, videos, etc. in databases, shared drives, social media, etc. However, to share

tacit knowledge effectively is more elusive. Some suggest that you hire smart people and let them talk to each other. Similarly, organizations create ways for people to communicate and collaborate such as social networks, conferences, organizational "water cooler" spaces for people to talk, or providing "knowledge maps" to search for people with needed expertise. However, as will be discussed in Chapter 4, this also requires a culture of trust, relationships and collaboration.
5. Knowledge application: Finally, how do you use this knowledge effective for innovation and resulting competitive advantage? This is not a passive activity. Most knowledge research professionals agree that it takes a dedicated effort with a CKO (Chief Knowledge Officer) or similar to plan, coordinate, manage and implement these activities. It also requires a culture of collaboration, continual learning, trust and a quest for knowledge and continual improvement. Finally, it requires leadership who are sincerely engaged in the entire effort behind this and who will work to create the culture and resources necessary to make it happen.

There have been many research studies showing a positive correlation between knowledge-intensive activities and resulting innovation in organizations. This includes the creation of new knowledge by combining internal and external knowledge (Trantopoulos et al., 2017). In their research, these authors confirmed the critical role that knowledge transfer plays in continual process innovation, leading to organizational competitive advantage where they used the

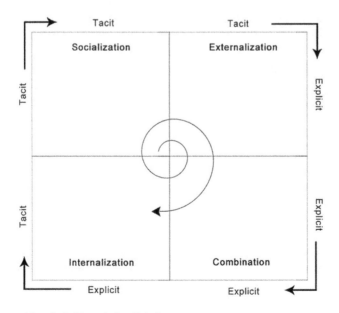

FIGURE 2.1 Nonaka's Knowledge Spiral

26 Explosive Innovation

well-established EUROSTAT Community Innovation Survey (CIS) in Swiss manufacturing firms. Their results showed quantitative improvement in proxy measures such as cost reductions and process improvements.

A similar study by Nitzsche et al. (2016) examined the success factors for innovation and competitive advantage. They reiterate the resource-based theory from a plethora of research showing that rare, non-imitable resources; primarily unique knowledge that is effectively shared, is the major sources of continual new knowledge and innovation in the firm. They discuss the need for organizations to be continually open and proactive in learning and seeking new knowledge, similar to our stories about combat troops that survive by continual learning and training. They further discuss that an organization's culture is crucial to supporting and nurturing this attitude of continual learning and knowledge acquisition. This is further inter-related to the concept of absorptive capacity, where innovation continues as people continue to learn and build upon their prior knowledge. Another important factor involves flexibility and the ability to network and share crucial knowledge from different fields and perspectives.

An interesting study by Perez and Soto (2017) looked at the role of innovation in small and medium size enterprises (SMEs), especially given the increasingly dynamic nature of change in virtually all business environments. The literature supports the view that these firms are resource-challenged, and thus, at a competitive disadvantage in their ability to respond to these dynamic competitive pressures. They are usually not able to innovate on a sustained basis like larger organizations because of their resource deprivations. However, these authors also found that SMEs that adhered to a culture of continual learning and knowledge acquisition within and outside the organization, they were able to innovate on a continual basis and maintain a better competitive advantage in these dynamic markets. Interestingly, they suggest that several of the core success factors involved in these innovation activities include continual training, proactive idea generation, regular meetings and a focus on effective communication and collaboration and effective technologies to facilitate collaboration and knowledge sharing. An attitude and culture of continual learning and exploration of the external environment were also factors in sustainable innovation and competitive advantage.

Knowledge Management in Practice

Some things to consider on a more practical level:

1. Do you recall from personal experience ever receiving "bad" knowledge? As you reflect on this, what can you learn about recognizing "bad" (or "good") knowledge going forward?
2. In your industry over the last ten years, where have the major innovations come from—product or process?

3. From an innovation standpoint, what are your organization's strengths in innovating?
4. We have also talked about political–social and geographic innovation—do these offer opportunities for your organization in the competitive marketplace?
5. How "quick" are you at recognizing change in the competitive environment (recall the Sears example in this chapter)?

Veteran Quotes: What Our Veterans Had to Say About the Value of Putting Knowledge to Work

World War II and Korean War

- This Veteran was a combat infantry soldier in World War II and in the Korean War. He fought in the Battle of the Bulge in World War II as well as in many front-line battles in the Korean War, sharing his valuable knowledge learned in the trenches with his buddies to keep them all alive through teaching and mentoring. For example, he would take his squad of 12 men on patrol where he could share his experiences in the field. He had studied continually what the other patrols had done, especially when they had gotten ambushed, learned from that and adapted the strategies of his unit, and then shared this new knowledge with his troops. One interesting example was during the Battle of the Bulge. Because ammunition was in short supply, he taught his men how to listen for the sound and pattern of firing their guns during a battle so that they could fire in a controlled sequence to use the scarce ammunition as effectively as possible rather than wasting ammunition in chaotic "free for all" shooting. He also had earned the trust and respect of his troops so that he was able to share his knowledge to help them all survive the horrors of the battlefield and the harsh conditions in World War II and Korea.

Vietnam

- It was during the intense battles with the North Vietnamese at the time of the buildup in the mid-1960s when this Captain was told to take his unit and set up an ambush. From his prior tours of duty in Vietnam, he had learned some important lessons about the enemy and their tactics. He had also learned that to lead, you had to get to know your troops and to work hard to earn their respect and create an environment where they knew they could trust you. Based on his experience and his ability to share his valuable knowledge with his troops, the ambush was successful. However, in the retreat, he had not remembered to plan for the safety of fox holes when they were returning to their base. Because of this unanticipated exposure,

28 Explosive Innovation

two of his Soldiers were killed by the North Vietnamese, which would haunt him forever more. However, he did an after-action review (AAR) to share his new knowledge with about 20 guys who were involved in the action and to learn from what they saw and experienced to prevent this from happening to others.

- A small American unit was isolated by an enemy unit and the Captain was told to rescue them. The area had tall weeds, so it was difficult to see where his people were and where the enemy was. He had a "vision" of what he expected to find and what to do. This helped him to make a workable plan and he was thus able to land and rescue the surrounded unit. He does not know where the vision came from; but suspects that it was based on prior experience that enabled him to integrate past knowledge to create new knowledge that saved the lives of his unit and rescue the wounded troops.

- You need *trust* to share knowledge. For example in Vietnam, in a helicopter medevac unit, there were always two people and you had to have a great bond between these people. You would not let anybody fly a helicopter that was not safe. Therefore the pilots had to trust the maintenance people that the helicopters were safe to fly.

Global War on Terror (GWOT); Iraq

- Key leader engagement. One of the Veterans had a job where he went on missions with officers and met with many different local Iraq leaders of different villages and towns. They would have lunch/dinner with them and ask these leaders what they needed. They would talk about contracts if they needed things like jobs, water systems, etc. These local people were suspicious because their villages had been destroyed and they often had nothing left; no food, water, money, etc. Therefore, the mission was to work with them; to produce "satisfied customers" so that they did not go to the other side for these necessities of life. These local people needed to do what was necessary to feed and clothe their families. Therefore, the mission was to help fill these needs; pay them to do things, set up shops, repair the water systems, etc. This helped to improve their lives. In this job, he met a lot of different people at each meeting and learned a lot about the different cultures, language; learned to communicate with people from these different cultures and find common ground. This knowledge was crucial in helping them work with the local people; make the right decisions based on good knowledge so that the locals would not side with the enemy, but rather, would help our troops.

- Army Ranger Captain: There was an event in Mosul during his first deployment where he knew that if they stayed static, someone would fire on them. Because they would be out for 12 hours, he took the gunners position, looked around and put himself in the place of the enemy; he studied the area, the streets, the buildings, the positions where the enemy could attack from and make a getaway; this helped him anticipate where the enemy could shoot from; recognize the non-explicit cues. For example, he observed that when the neighborhood emptied out, that meant that the terrorist were preparing an attack, so he learned to be aware of clues like this. In fact, at one point, he observed this happening and the enemy did fire a rocket launcher attack at them. However, because he was aware of enemy tactics, they were prepared for it. Based on his experiences/acquired knowledge, he positioned his equipment and people in the best places and was able to successfully take out the enemy without losing any of his troops.

- There were snipers in the city, so you needed to learn how to detect/scan for them. He had to go out and do this to demonstrate to his people the dangers; establish credibility with his unit so that he could translate this new knowledge about the snipers to them so that they would understand and embrace this new knowledge. He also had to get them to understand that the enemy is human, so you can study, learn about them and anticipate what they will do.
- After-action reviews (especially with casualties): sit down with everyone and discuss what happened, what went wrong and what could have been done better to prevent the casualties.

GWOT; Afghanistan

- There is something called a "hot wash"; often known as an after-action review. There are kinetic or non-kinetic situations; kinetic being when a unit/person is tactically engaged or in a fire fight with the enemy and non-kinetic; when you are not engaged by the enemy. This information is provided by you and your fellow Marines to the intelligence officer or analyst who gathers information immediately after an operation from all units in this "hot wash" so that they can consolidate knowledge and use it to predict new situations.
- The sound of mortar fire is different between different rockets and there is also a unique time delay for the different rockets. This creates a baseline of knowledge, so you notice when something is different from the baseline. During a mission, they heard a new sound and the explosion was much faster than prior mortar rockets. After the attack, they sent a team to investigate and found the shells from the mortar and discovered that it was from a "SPG-9" (Pronounced SPIG-9) (see http://en.wikipedia.org/wiki/SPG-9) recoilless rifle, which was considered uncommon in the area at that point. However, they knew that this was a close-range weapon, which meant that the enemy had to be close by, which influenced their own strategies. In terms of new knowledge creation:

30 Explosive Innovation

- o You needed preparation to know that this weapon existed
- o You needed conscious awareness; to not be deterred by a new, unexpected weapon, but to think logically; the ability to think clearly and see the problem as it was.

- Sometimes you have to learn in the field. For example, in his first gunfight, he and his unit noticed that women and children were running from one building to another, but they did not know what this meant. They later learned that this was a signal that the enemy was going to attack. After this, they all understood these signals and could be better prepared for the enemy attack.
- One field unit found a lot of IEDs and their equipment did not help to detect them, so someone came up with a new technique; a low-tech, low cost method that worked pretty well. Since it would have taken a long time for official channels to come up with a more sophisticated method, this new technique (new knowledge) was communicated throughout their unit. Then, since people all knew each other within the larger unit, they would tell their friends and it would be transferred by word-of-mouth pretty quickly. This was because these Marines cared about their friends, had developed close friendships and wanted to keep their friends safe.

References

Andrews, E. (2014). "8 Things You May Not Know About the Battle of the Bulge", History.com, available at www.history.com/news/8-things-you-may-not-know-about-the-battle-of-the-bulge (accessed September 25, 2016).

Berkun, S. (2013). "The Best Definition of Innovation", available at http://scottberkun.com/2013/the-best-definition-of-innovation/ (accessed August 1, 2016).

Cokins, G. (2015). "Why Once-Successful Companies Fail," Information Management blog, January 6, available at www.information-management.com/blogs/Business-Failure-Success-Analytics-10026399-1.html (accessed August 1, 2016).

Delaney, B. (2013). "$10,000 Cervelo Rca Frame That Weighs 667g—First Look and Ride", available at www.bikeradar.com/us/road/news/article/10000-cervelo-rca-frame-that-weighs-667g-first-look-and-ride-36710/ (accessed February 2, 2017).

Elmansy, R. (N.D.). "Design Thinking Case Study: Innovation at Apple", Designorate, available at www.designorate.com/design-thinking-case-study-innovation-at-apple/ (accessed August 23, 2016).

Hetherington, S. (2008). "Knowing-that, knowing-how, and knowing philosophically", *Grazer Philosophische Studien*, Vol. 77 No.1: 307–324.

Hubbard, B. and Schmitt, E. (2014). "Military Skill and Terrorist Technique Fuel Success of ISIS", *New York Times*, available at www.nytimes.com/2014/08/28/world/middleeast/army-know-how-seen-as-factor-in-isis-successes.html?_r=0 (accessed March 23, 2016).

Leonard-Barton, D. (1995). *Wellsprings of Knowledge: Building and Sustaining the Sources of Innovation*. Cambridge, MA: Harvard Business School Press.

Lutz, A. (2015). "A Troubling Sign That Sears Is Close to Death", BusinessInsider.com, available at www.businessinsider.com/sears-sales-decline-2015-8 (accessed July 9, 2016).

Nitzsche, P., Wirtz, B. and Gottel, V. (2016). "Innovation success in the context of inbound open innovation", *International Journal of Innovation Management*, Vol. 20 No. 2: 1–38.

Nonaka, I. and Takeuchi, N. (1995). *The Knowledge-Creating Company: How Japanese Companies Create the Dynamics of Innovation*. New York: Oxford University Press.

Perez-Soltero, A. and Soto, V. L. (2017). "A model based on core processes and knowledge management to promote innovation: A case of a Mexican trading company", *Journal of Knowledge Management*, Vol. 15 No. 1: 7–29.

Peters, T. and Waterman, R. J. (1989). *In Search of Excellence: Lessons from America's Best-Run Companies*. New York: Warner Books.

Power, D. (2016). "What Are Examples of Bad Strategic Business Decisions?", available at http://dssresources.com/faq/index.php?action=artikel&id=318 (accessed August 23, 2016).

Sweeney, B. (2012). "Sears—Where America Shopped", available at www.chicagobusiness.com/article/20120421/ISSUE01/304219970/sears-where-america-shopped (accessed July 7, 2016).

Thon, S. and Steinhauser, L. (2009). "Knowledge Transfer Through People", United States Strategic Command Knowledge Transfer Office, available at http://usacac.army.mil/cac2/AOKM/Knowledge%20Transfer%20Book.pdf (accessed September 3, 2016).

Trantopoulos, K., von Krogh, G., Wallin, M. W. and Woerter, M. (2017). "External knowledge and information technology: Implications for process innovation performance", *MIS Quarterly*, Vol. 41 No. 1: 287–109.

U.S. Army Center of Military History. (2011). "Battle of the Bulge", available at https://history.army.mil/html/reference/bulge/index.html (accessed September 25, 2016).

3

LEADERSHIP

Geniuses and prophets do not usually excel in professional learning, and their originality, if any, is often due precisely to the fact that they do not.

—Joseph Alois Schumpeter

The best leaders . . . almost without exception and at every level, are master users of stories and symbols.

—Tom Peters

There is an enormous amount of books and articles on leadership and we cannot possibly distil all of their lessons in a single book, much less a single chapter. What is important to note is the link here between leadership, innovation and knowledge management. There are numerous questionnaires and experiential exercises that one can use to explore and assess leadership. In addition, we continue to provide brief comments from Veterans we interviewed regarding this topic of leadership which can be found at the end of this chapter. Leadership is often a combination of the situation and the individual where critical thinking and decision-making are demanded in unique and rapidly unfolding situations.

Colonel Joshua Chamberlain, a former minister and Bowdoin professor found himself in just such a unique situation. The 20th Maine, the unit that he commanded, sat on the top of Little Round Top at the Battle of Gettysburg. Although historians differ on the significance of the location there was concern that if the 15th Alabama under the command of Colonel William Oates seized the position, it might allow the Confederate Army to "sweep the Union line" and potentially win the battle. What actually happened and the strength of the Confederate forces has been subjected to debate. What is clear is that after several charges up hill, the 15th Alabama was exhausted (and without replacement water). What is also clear is that the 20th Maine ran out of ammunition. Chamberlain, concerned about potentially losing Little Round Top, ordered his men to fix bayonets (there is also some dispute over whether or not he actually ordered a charge).

The net result was that Chamberlain's troops swept down the hill (momentum being on their side) and caught the Confederate forces by surprise. This bold move enabled the Union to hold on to Little Round Top and cemented Chamberlain as a "war hero". Later, in recognition for this and other battlefield successes, General Grant appointed Chamberlain to preside over the surrender of arms by the Confederate Army at Appomattox. As the defeated Confederate soldiers and officers passed the Union troops on either side of the road, Chamberlain ordered his troops to present arms, a final salute to those who fought on the other side.

Chamberlain acted decisively at the battle of Little Round Top, engaging, as we have noted, in an unusual attack where there was no existing manual or procedure that offered insight as to what one should do. The key was that he made a decision when it was needed, and exercised leadership at a moment when decisive leadership was needed (Chamberlain, 1889; Desjardin, 1995; Longacre and Chamberlain, 2003; McPherson, 2003; LaFantasie, 2008; —for the more visual learner, this entire episode was depicted in the popular movie *Gettsyburg*, 1993).

What do leaders do, broadly stated? Leaders (1) set the tone and culture of an organization (and we will look at culture in the next chapter; (2) have the power and authority to establish rewards, incentives and punishments as well as to allocate resources in the organization; (3) are generally recognized to be smart, motivated, care about and can inspire their people, can see the big picture and develop a shared mission and vision for the organization. That is, they tend to be both task and people-oriented; (4) some of our prior research has shown that leaders must be trustworthy individuals who establish a culture of respect and knowledge sharing, and who value the attainment of the organizational mission and goals over personal power or political agendas; and (5) as noted above with General Chamberlain leaders need to be flexible and adapt to changing situations and circumstances.

What is emerging and "new" about leadership is that it is unwise to focus on one individual within an organization as the embodiment of leadership. Leadership is being increasingly recognized as a broader skill within the organization that can be found in top management teams and in the skillful use of groups and teams to achieve organizational purposes up and down the organization (Finkelstein et al., 2009; Charlier et al., 2016). Therefore, when we refer to leadership here, we include both examples of individual leaders and leadership teams and groups and recognize that leadership can, and should be exercised at any level in the organization.

A major consistent observation from the *Fortune 500* list of Most Admired Corporations is that these particular firms are well led and seek out innovation at every opportunity. Although we have not noted it previously, innovation is either a severe threat to existing businesses and industries or an incredible opportunity. Consider the explorations being undertaken today in wind, solar and

34 Leadership

tidal power—if they come to fruition what does this mean for the future of the petroleum industry? W. Edwards Deming once observed that "Learning is not compulsory . . . neither is survival." These challenges require BOTH an innovation approach and leadership that supports and nourishes it as shown in the boxed insert.

Just What is Leadership?

Stephen Hawking, the holder of the Lucasian Professorship of Mathematics at Cambridge University (a chair once held by Issac Newton) once famously observed that "leadership is daring to take a step into the unknown". Although this is a provocative and inspirational definition, it does not help us fully understand what leadership is, how it is "obtained" or more importantly how it is exercised. We have, as a society, been fascinated with leadership, how it is possessed or developed and to what ends it is used. There is simply not enough space to review all the literature on leadership—so what follows is a brief overview of some of the major works in leadership.

We can trace the beginning of leadership studies in a more formal sense back to Plato (Jowett, 1892) who wanted to address what qualities or aspects make a person a leader (although Plato did not always use this term, often referring to leaders as "guardians"). As might be expected, in the Middle Ages, leadership was often seen as the province of the royal class, of kings and queens, and therefore easily encapsulated as hereditary. This led to an easy (and erroneous conclusion) that leadership was, in fact, hereditary (see Carlyle, 1841; Galton, 1869). Cecil Rhodes decided to focus his efforts on understanding leadership by looking at leadership in the public sector and funding, upon his death, the internationally renowned Rhodes Scholarships in 1903.

The trait view of leadership was subsequently replaced by investigations into the behaviors of leaders that were particularly effective, that is, that we could define leadership by behaviors. This approach recognized that leadership might be effective in some situations and not in others (Stogdill, 1948). But the traits approach to defining leadership was not to be denied, and with the growth of scholarship in the leadership area, statistical methodology and research design, traits as the basis for understanding leadership was reinvigorated (see Kenny and Zaccaro, 1983; Lord et al., 1986; Kickul and Neuman, 2000). However, trait based approaches were still subjected to criticisms. Zaccaro (2007) raised numerous problems relating to both the methodological approaches used in such studies, the stability of such traits over time and the failure to consider such influencing factors as social skills, decision-making skills and values in shaping leadership. Despite this, there remains a strong thread of leadership research that examines traits of leaders.

Another school of thought in leadership studies has looked at contingency theories—arguing that a leader is more a function of the situation than the reverse. According to Hemphill (1949) what a person does in terms of leadership is really a function of the specific situation that the individual is facing (recall the earlier example of Chamberlain). Additional support for this view is found in the works of Fiedler (1967; 1981) and what he identified as situational contingencies. In his works he argued that there are really two types of leaders, and this view has gained great visibility and support in organizational life. According to Fiedler, one type of leader is oriented to completion of the task at hand, to getting the assigned job done—what he called task focused leadership. The other type of leader is one who achieves success by focusing on relationships with others. Fiedler noted that there was no one, absolute ideal leader approach. But as you consider your own leadership style, what do you tend to emphasize—task performance or relationships, or do you vary between the two as the specific situation demands? What about your boss? How would your subordinates identify your leadership style?

As you can see, there are numerous approaches to understanding and studying leadership. Other views include: a path-goal model which allows for different leadership styles and approaches based on the needs of the situation (House, 1996); functional theory approaches which emphasize leaders' actions and behaviors that contribute to organizational effectiveness (Kouzes and Posner, 1995); and even servant leadership approaches where it is recognized that the leader is a servant of those s/he leads (Greenleaf, 2002; Greenleaf and Spears, 2002).

But the question still remains, what do we mean by leadership? The Oxford Dictionary offers the following: "the action of leading a group of people or an organization" or "the state or position of being a leader" (https://en.oxforddictionaries. com/definition/leadership). This definition is representative of numerous works that define leadership. Investopedia offers a more focused definition of leadership that we find more helpful in an organizational context. They define leadership as:

> the ability of a company's management to set and achieve challenging goals, take swift and decisive action, outperform the competition, and inspire others to perform well.
>
> *(www.investopedia.com/terms/l/leadership.asp)*

Look closely at this and other definitions of leadership. A concern is that there is not always a clear recognition of the goals being pursued and their value. For example, someone who incites a crowd to riot would be seen as a leader—but the purpose of this "leadership" would certainly be subjected to criticism. Therefore, in our view, leadership, while intellectually definable as noted above cannot be divorced by the consequences of the actions and results of that leadership.

Leadership in Organizations

The driving question for leadership in organization is how to harness innovation on a continual basis and to use groups and teams to foster and develop the culture (discussed in the next chapter) of a constantly innovative organization that uses knowledge adroitly, consistently and well. The late and very creative Steve Jobs captured this approach in his observation that:

36 Leadership

> Innovation has nothing to do with how many R&D dollars you have. When Apple came up with the Mac, IBM was spending at least 100 times more on R&D. It's not about money. It's about the people you have, how you're led, and how much you get it.
>
> *(Kahn, 2011)*

It should be clear that leadership is a crucial component of, and contributor to, innovation in organizations. The use of teams and groups to innovate and develop new products is also becoming a necessary condition for innovation in large organizations. Tracy Kidder (1981) in his Pulitzer Prize-winning work, *The Soul of a New Machine*, captured the challenges of innovation in the high technology industry documenting in detail the struggles internally in Data General's attempt to build a new 32-bit microcomputer in one year. This work recounts the leadership of a group of people within the firm who did not receive authorization to develop the new microcomputer. They worked on it on their own time and, fortunately for Data General, this team succeeded where the team authorized to develop the new product failed. Another example of team based success is shown in the boxed insert.

When Stanley Works merged with Black & Decker Corp. in 2010, it inherited a floundering power-tool unit. "We were losing our way", says John Cunningham, president of the consumer products division of Stanley Black & Decker Inc., who had been with Dewalt, part of Black & Decker, before the merger. "As we changed leadership, we were faced with turning the brand around and reinvigorating it."

One of the new leadership team's first moves: carve out innovation teams freed of daily time-to-market pressures. Now one team based in Maryland focuses on applying new technology to current products and a second one in the U.K. develops what Cunningham characterizes as "disruptive technologies". They're given time, money and regular access to senior leaders.

"Give me the solution", Cunningham tells them. "I'll make the decision about whether we can make money at this idea."

One of the first hits: a motion-activated screwdriver. The Black & Decker Gyro grew from a Maryland engineer's curiosity about applying the concept behind a Nintendo Wii controller to a screwdriver. *Time* magazine dubbed it "one of the best inventions of the year".

Stanley Black & Decker and others know that clinging to convention can be fatal. That's why innovation has become the top priority of CEOs worldwide. More than 80 percent of respondents to a recent Workforce survey said innovation had become much more important to their organizations and they expected it to remain so (Henneman, 2013).

But how do we do this? Dyer et al. (2009; 2013) have suggested the following framework as a starting point for leadership in innovative organizations:

1. Innovative leaders tend to have five "discovery skills": associating, questioning, observing, networking and experimenting.
2. Leaders seeking to foster an innovative workforce should focus first on demonstrating these behaviors themselves. "Walking the talk when it comes to innovation is critical", he says.
3. Don't expect big results overnight. Building a culture of productive innovation—where employees practice the five discovery skills—takes time. Just opening the floor to suggestions can lead to a flood of low-value proposals. "Those organizations will get lots of ideas, but most of them aren't worth pursuing."
4. Less is more when it comes to team size. A group of six to eight people— a team that can be fed by two pizzas—is best for solving tough problems. Larger groups can get bogged down in bureaucracy. "Big problems often get tackled by small teams in innovative companies."
5. Build trust and develop relationships so that people will feel comfortable and willing to share their valuable knowledge and collaborate.

Once again we see the emphasis on the use of teams or groups in organizations to pursue innovation—but how do we use teams effectively? Cheong et al. (2016) warn that empowering leadership in subordinates also imposes burdens that are not always understood or considered by managers.

Vroom and Yetton's research (1973) is a useful aid to us in deciding *when* and *how* to use groups. Their model is a decision tree in which managers address a series of seven questions regarding their current situation (see boxed insert)—we have substituted "leader" for "manager" in their original formulation and have modified the categories to address innovation specifically. It was originally developed to aid in the overall decision-making process but we believe it has direct implication for the leadership decisions associated with innovation teams and in the management of knowledge.

A. Is there a quality requirement such that one solution is likely to prove more rational than another? If it matters what alternative is selected there must be a quality requirement and the leader should be involved.

B. Does the leader have sufficient information to make a high quality decision? If the leader does not have sufficient information to make the decision, he or she should involve subordinates who may have the relevant information or expertise needed.

(continued)

38 Leadership

(continued)

C. Is the problem structured? If the problem is ambiguous (and this is a challenge for innovation) the leader should work with subordinates to help clarify the problem and suggest potential reasonable alternative solutions/approaches.
D. Is acceptance of the decision by others (including subordinates) in the organization critical to implementation? If the innovation requires the support of others to understand, develop and act on the innovation, it is crucial that they are involved. We see this as a major weakness in organizations—that innovation is not pursued with the actual implementation of that innovation clearly understood.
E. If the leader were to make the decision by him or herself is it reasonably certain that it would be accepted by subordinates and others and that it would actually be, and be seen as, innovative? As noted above (and as evidenced in Kidder's (1981) work noted earlier), subordinate involvement in and acceptance of the leader's actions and decisions with regards to innovation is critical.
F. Do subordinates (and others) share in, understand and support the organizational goals to be obtained in development of this innovation? If the answer is no, the leader has two challenges—to communicate more clearly the need for innovation and to ensure that subordinates do not make decisions or act contrarily to the innovation process unfolding.
G. Is conflict likely in the organization with regards to the selected innovation and/or the innovation process itself? If conflict is likely, the leader will need to remain involved in the process to resolve conflicts.

Vroom and Yetton (1973) used these questions to develop a decision tree for making decisions to involve groups and teams and at what level of involvement (and as an exercise can you build a decision tree for your use from this information). At one extreme, the leader announces a decision and subordinates are expected to accept and implement it. At the other extreme (often found in attempts at innovation) the leader notes the need for innovation, and leaves the group/team to search and develop the innovation (the Black & Decker approach noted earlier)—what is sometimes referred to as "loose leadership", defined as giving space for new ideas and exploration (DuBrin, 2016). This giving of space must recognize that there will be false starts and that such actions should not be penalized if the goal is to encourage innovative and creative thinking.

Even recognized talented leaders make mistakes. Warren Buffett is acknowledged for his genius in the identification of companies that are going to be very successful in the future and investing in them and reaping rich returns. But in 1993 he made, for him, what he termed his biggest mistake.

Leadership **39**

In 1993 Buffett and his partner Charlie Munger bought the Dexter Shoe Company which was located in a small town in Maine. Buffett touted the superb management of the company and paid $433 million for it. In 2008, Buffett observed that it was "the worst deal that I've made". Buffett was caught by the erosion of the Dexter Shoe Company's competitive advantage, and the overtaking of innovations that Dexter had championed. Even more "hurtful" was that the purchase was made with Berkshire Hathaway stock (not cash), and the result was, given the appreciation of the stock, that the true cost of the purchase was not $433 million but $3.5 billion. What makes this story so unique is that Buffett publicly acknowledged his mistake (a rarity among leaders of any organization) and understood the reasons why he was wrong. An interesting aspect of the leadership of Berkshire Hathaway is that there has been zero turnover in the top leadership of the organization. As Hallinan (2009) notes, this might explain their extraordinary performance—between 1964 and 2007 the company reported an overall gain of 400,863% (and Standard and Poor's 500 Index, including dividends, gained only 6,840% over the same time period). We should note, however, that there is a difference between leaders who make bad decisions (as all do on occasion) and bad leadership (Nassar et al., 2016).

Here is a view on leadership and innovation from a Veteran we interviewed; a Sergeant in the tank unit in Iraq:

> It was 2003, at the very start of the Iraq War. The unit of tanks was among one of the first going in to take Bagdad. Just as the unit was preparing to start the offensive, the commander of this unit came over to the tank of Sargeant S. said "I can't do this" and just left, leaving Sergeant S. as the highest ranking person in that unit. One important fact behind this is that Sergeant S. was with the combat maintenance unit, which would normally be right behind the infantry to support them. He had two choices. He could turn leadership of the offensive over to a younger, less experienced officer or he could take on the leadership role. Because he had the best knowledge of his unit rather than an infantry person who did not know anything about them, he decided that he was the best person to keep them going. He also knew that the Soldiers would not necessarily trust or respect the authority of the young, inexperienced Lieutenant. Therefore, Sergeant S. made the crucial decision in a split second to take charge of the entire unit: combat infantry and combat maintenance.

It took them about 14 days to get to Baghdad and no one got any sleep during that time. By chance, their unit was the first to enter the combat zone: "his guys were freaking out". How did his unit end up getting there first? It had to do with bad leadership.

They had gotten to a section which they called "little Vietnam" with palm trees and mud everywhere because an officer (Major) forced them into this area and got

40 Leadership

most of them stuck in the mud because he did not understand what would happen when they tried to get through this muddy area with their tanks and heavy equipment. However, Sergeant S.'s tank was one of the few that did *not* get stuck in the mud although everyone else did so they ended up on the front lines of the battle. How did he know how to get them through the mud? He looked at the terrain. He had been through recovery school where he learned how to deal with muddy conditions and was able to guide people through but the others did not because they had not had that type of training. In the end, his prior knowledge from training and his knowledge of his people helped them get through that terrible battle.

There were about 1,000 of them versus about 2,000 Iraqis. Even though Sergeant S.'s unit had gotten through the mud to the front of the line, everyone else was still stuck in the mud, fighting all night. The battle was fierce. The Marines were in the reeds in hand-to-hand combat with bayonets. Later, they would learn from Lieutenant Colonel Marcone, "The amazing part was that we didn't realize how big the force we were fighting, and it was one tank company that fought that brigade. He never called for reinforcements" (Armchair General, 2003).

During that time, Sergeant S. reported that he "found himself"; he discovered his leadership skills and learned about human nature. He learned to listen to and get to know what his people could do in order to make good decisions based on knowledge of the capabilities of his unit.

Another famous leadership failure was Stalin:

> Months before the Germans invaded Russia in 1941, Soviet military intelligence reported their intentions. Later, the British sent a warning that they too had discovered the preparations for Operation Barbarossa. The top Russian spy in Japan even reported details of the plan that had been shared with the Nazi ally. Stalin stubbornly insisted it was all just a plot by the British to involve him in the war. Since disagreeing with Stalin was consistently fatal, no one dared to tell him differently. Even with over two million Wehrmacht soldiers poised on his frontier, Stalin reacted by telling his commanders to avoid provoking the Germans. In the next two months, millions of Russian soldiers and civilians paid for his mistake with their lives.
>
> *(Fawcett, 2014)*

The challenge for leaders is to simultaneously communicate their knowledge to the rest of the organization, to ensure that processes exist to extract knowledge from all their employees and to ensure that there are processes in place to develop, transfer and share knowledge across the organization in a timely fashion and on a continuous basis. This is not an easy task, but it does demonstrate the value in using teams and groups as the members of the teams/groups can serve to communicate new discoveries faster than a single individual.

For example, in August of 1949 there was a horrific forest fire in Mann Gulch, Montana. Thirteen firefighters (smoke jumpers as they were known) parachuted into the area and died in that fire. It was the worst disaster in the history of the American Forest Service.

Wagner Dodge, the supervisor, survived because he did something no one had thought of, which was not part of the training or contained in any Forest Service instruction manuals—an example of tacit knowledge and innovation in the heat of the moment. He saved himself (and tried to get the others to follow his example without success) by setting what was termed an "escape fire". Forest Service experts, after the fire, noted that they had never heard of an escape fire. What Dodge did was convert tacit knowledge to action, but sadly he was unable to convince his colleagues that his actions were correct:

> When he (Dodge) tried to explain this (to the crew), it was too late—no one understood him . . . his escape fire had only one kind of value—the value of thought of a fire foreman in time of emergency judged purely as thought.
>
> *(Maclean, 1992, p. 102)*

Another example of an individual exercising leadership and innovation in times of crisis is Captain Chesley Sullenberger's landing of a plane on the Hudson River in New York in January of 2015. All 155 passengers and crew survived (and this has been documented in the movie *Sully*). For a more in-depth look at the investigations into the crash and a deeper understanding of the tacit knowledge and innovation based in this situation see Sullenberger and Zaslow, 2010. In this situation, he encountered something new and unique and had to use his accumulated knowledge and experiences from 29 years as a pilot. In his autobiography he writes,

> Sullenberger's years of airline safety instruction and study paid off on January 15, 2009, when the US Airways plane he was piloting struck a large flock of Canada geese during liftoff from New York's LaGuardia Airport. Both engines were damaged, and suddenly neither was providing any thrust. With air traffic control, Sullenberger discussed his options: either return to LaGuardia or land at Teterboro Airport in New Jersey. Sullenberger quickly deemed the situation too dire for the plane to stay in the air long enough for either plan to be successful, so he decided that ditching (performing an emergency water landing) the jet in the Hudson River was the best option.
>
> *(biography.com, undated)*

Leadership, as we have tried to portray in this chapter, is a combination of the individual, the group and the situation at hand. Leadership is necessary for organizations, for innovation and for knowledge management, but it is but one aspect, and culture is yet another important component of both innovation and knowledge management.

42 Leadership

Leadership in Practice

1. How would you define your leadership orientation? Are you task focused? Are you relationship focused?
2. Consider a leader you admire; why do you admire them? What is it that they do or say that merits your approval and support?
3. Can you, in a team-based context, switch between roles of leader and member of the team?
4. Consider a recent situation in which you observed a failure of leadership. What contributed to that failure?
5. What concrete actions are you taking to keep your leadership skills current?

What Did We Learn From the Veterans?

There have been a "million" books and articles written about leadership and business. What have we learned from these Veterans about leadership that can help businesses?

1. Establish a mission and vision for the organization that you believe is valuable and communicate it clearly to everyone. E.g. everyone needs to truly believe in the mission and vision in order to develop the trust and relationships to work as a team.
2. Be a "servant" leader (Greenleaf and Spears, 2002; Sipe and Frick, 2015):

    a. Be someone who "walks the walk"; is willing to "go into the trenches" and do anything that he or she would ask any of their people to do.
    b. Be humble; be the person who truly cares about your people.
    c. Build in the time to listen and learn what your people have to say. Take the time to understand your people as well as their jobs. This will help establish real credibility with your team.
    d. Understand how the organization is run; its challenges and opportunities.

3. Proactively develop a culture that mirrors this "servant leadership" attitude; communicate the mission and vision so that all associates understand what everyone is trying to accomplish and their role in the big picture.
4. Develop a culture of *respect and trust*. Each person plays a valuable role in achieving the mission and vision. Make sure that everyone is recognized and feels valued and appreciated for their role and contributions. Be a mentor who empowers your people; make them feel valued, involved, appreciated; recognize their accomplishment towards achievement of the mission and tasks.
5. Set high expectations for everyone to achieve the mission and vision. Hold everyone to these high standards in a collaborative team environment. Make sure that managers are involved with their teams; know their teams, provide active guidance and feedback.

Leadership **43**

6. Establish a reward-incentive system that encourages communication, collaboration and attainment of the organizational goals, mission and vision. Make sure that metrics and measurements support each person and team's efforts to contribute to the overall goals, mission and vision.
7. Give people real responsibility, authority and accountability, but "have their back" to support them and help them succeed. Hold them to high standards, but let them know what the expectations are.
8. Develop and maintain a positive, can-do attitude. By staying positive and keeping an open mind, a good leader can listen and truly understand what people are saying in order to communicate well and adapt to changing conditions.

Leadership Resources

Experiential Exercises

These are fun and can be helpful, but no one in our view is better than another:

1. How good are your leadership skills? A self-assessment tool at www.mindtools.com/pages/article/newLDR_50.htm
2. The Blake and Mouton Managerial Grid for assessing leadership style based on task or relationship focus at www.bumc.bu.edu/facdev-medicine/files/2010/10/Leadership-Matrix-Self-Assessment-Questionnaire.pdf
3. TSCE Leadership Style Questionnaire for self-assessment at www.stellarleadership.com/docs/Leadership/assessment/TSCE%20Leadership%20Style%20Questionnaire.pdf
4. Your leadership legacy at www.yourleadershiplegacy.com/assessment/assessment.php
5. Leadership Matrix survey at www.nwlink.com/~donclark/leader/matrix.html
6. Kaagan, Stephen S. (1998). *Leadership Games: Experiential Learning for Organizational Development*. Sage Publications.

Journal, Blog and Articles

1. *The Leadership Quarterly*. A journal that focuses specifically on leadership, its practical implications from a multi-disciplinary perspective (www.journals.elsevier.com/the-leadership-quarterly/).
2. *The Leadership Circle*. A blog dealing with leadership (https://leadershipcircle.com/resources/leadership-quarterly/).
3. Lopes, M. C., Fialho, F. A. P., Cunha, C. J. C. A and Niveiros, S. I. (2013). "Business games for leadership development: A systematic review." *Simulation & Gaming*, Vol. 44 No. 4: 523–543.

44 Leadership

4. Dentico, J. P. (1999). "Games leaders play: Using process simulations to develop collaborative leadership practices for a knowledge-based society." *Career Development International*, Vol. 4 No. 3: 175–182.

Veteran Quotes: Veterans' Perspectives on Leadership

In our conversations with Veterans, some of the things we learned about leadership from their experiences include the following.

World War II and Korea

- Don't be afraid of taking advice, listening; value what people have to say, especially your subordinates.
- Terrible leaders: autocratic, "know it all", self-absorbed, arrogant.
- Situational leadership and personality are also important.
- Credibility is crucial in developing trust and respect from those you command.
- Mentoring: he would routinely put PFCs in charge for a while to test them. He would first explain things to them for about a month and then gave them freedom to try it out. They enjoyed it. He would watch them closely—both in World War II and Korea.

Vietnam

- It makes it easy to lead when the leader and the members of the leader's group know what to expect and feel confident in the leader's decisions and the leader, the group's actions.
- Over half of his recon platoon had been with him for over a year in November 1965 and felt comfortable and confident with each other. They knew what to expect from each other. A good leader must know what to expect his subordinates to do in the absence of instructions.
- He feels strongly that the success of any organization is based on subordinates. These are the people who are going to make the business successful. The people who work for you need to know and do their job well. He says you must recognize that everyone is important and the leader has to make sure that everyone is recognized and valued.
- A mark of a leader—when you enter an organization, you need to learn as much as possible about that organization and the people who are serving under you. Don't try to make major change immediately unless it's a crisis. If so, let your experience guide you to do what seems to be correct.
- Being humble is part of being a true leader; someone who can stay in the background but their people know they are there and available and that they know what is going on. A good leader also recognizes everyone's personality and their contributions to the team.

- The "my way or the highway" approach will *not* work.
- People under your command need to feel comfortable with you and you also had to feel comfortable and confident with them. They had learned enough so that he knew what to expect from them. It makes it easy to lead if you have confidence in each other.
- The people who work for you need to do their job well. Also recognize that everyone is important and the leader has to make sure that everyone is recognized and valued.
- He received a letter years after retiring from the Army from one of his Lieutenants who said, "You knew us, knew our jobs, checked us and that was key to your success"; e.g. caring, knowing, learning, admitting mistakes. You see good people, bad people, and you learn from them; continual learning—don't get complacent.
- He worked as a mentor to the younger troops. He became a Platoon Sergeant of a gun platoon in Vietnam. As a First Sergeant he instilled in the troops that he would not ask them to do anything that he would not do for himself.
- Some qualities of a good leader are that they are humble, grounded, care about their people, and do whatever it takes to get the job done.
- Trust, respect, consistency, clear standards and expectations were crucial in the success of knowledge transfer in combat as well as in non-combat situations. Be straight and clear with people. Leaders really need to care about their people and they need to work with them to make them understand what they need to do and how to do it.
- E7: he was the production control NCO on the flight line. He took over the company. Then a new First Sergeant came in who had a "know it all" attitude and did not want to learn from him. In other words, there was no knowledge transfer even though this gentleman had a lot of knowledge to share that would have been helpful. The new NCO lasted a little while and then was transferred out of the unit. Trust, respect, consistency, clear standards and expectations were crucial in the success of knowledge transfer in combat as well as in non-combat situations. Be straight and clear with people.

Global War on Terror (GWOT); Iraq

- Leadership; getting to know human nature; learn to make decisions based on what his people could do.
- He put himself out there to gain information; he gained knowledge over time to develop this intuition. The most decisive point is the point of danger, so you gain this intuition and you develop a "sixth sense" so that when the decision-maker is at the point of attack, you are able to make decisions rapidly to prevent casualties. You develop the ability to anticipate and detect danger.

46 Leadership

- Back in 2003 at the very start of the Iraq War, they were the one of the first units going in. They encountered the first enemy bunker in the first 15 minutes. When they got to Iraq and were the first ones there his guys were "freaking out". It took them about 14 days to get to Baghdad and no one got any sleep during that time. During that time he found himself; his leadership; getting to know human nature. Therefore he learned to make decisions based on what his people could do.
- Physical leadership: showing your Soldiers (employees) your concern with actions rather than words. Being immersed and involved with them also allows you to learn a great deal about your Soldiers. Empathy helps you to learn more. The Soldiers knew that he would never ask them to do anything he would not do himself, which inspired them to do their jobs well. Empathy and sincere concern is a critical cog in the wheel.

GWOT; Afghanistan

- After the knowledge is shared, it will depend on the leadership and culture of the new unit on whether and how much of that knowledge they will choose to use or whether they prefer to do things their own way. But most units heavily rely on the lessons learned from the previous unit to continue with the successes already gained by their actions in that area. While most people will be good leaders and Marines, there may be a small minority of people who may not listen to the outgoing unit, may do things based on their own ideas and experiences even if it may not be the best way.
- Someone who has the ability to inspire and is willing to perform the menial tasks at the level of his subordinates. It is a person who is willing to learn about his people that gains respect from his people. In the story of Henry V, the king dressed as a commoner to learn what the people of his kingdom thought of him. Also, a leader that brings his team into the mindset of a collective mentality draws in a community-based organization. Example, "This is what needs to get done and how can we accomplish this?" Versus "You need to get this task done and this is how you are going to do it." Why? What is the end result? Why are you not doing it? What if I have a better way of doing it?
- There should be task and purpose: reward and encourage positive behaviors; not micromanage. Bad leaders tend to be self-entitled.
- Sometimes you have to learn in the field. For example, in his first gunfight, he and his unit noticed that women and children were running from one building to another, but they did not know what this meant. They later learned that this was a signal that the enemy was going to attack. After this, they all understood these signals.
- Leadership: making good decisions under pressure and communicating well. For example, if you are in a crisis situation, you only have one

Leadership **47**

radio channel, but need to communicate many things (e.g. tending to the wounded, getting air or ground support, communicating with your unit, etc.), the leader needs to be able to assess the situation, determine what is most important (priorities), keep the communications short and direct, and keep everyone's roles clear and structured in the communications. E.g. determine what information is most important and communicate each piece of important information to the correct person. Also, you need to understand the communication structure so that the most important information gets sent up the chain to the people who need it the most: such as air support, supervisors, command center, etc. and also send important information down the chain to people who need it such as medical, infantry, etc. Therefore, training and structure are very important. Training in communication, the hierarchy and how information flows most effectively and efficiently to accomplish the mission are very important. Do you know who to communicate information to?

- Leaders are both made and born. For example, you can have someone who has the height and reflexes to be a good basketball player, but does not have the interest or motivation. In contrast, you can have someone who is passionate about basketball, but does not have the height and reflexes to be a great player. Therefore, as discussed on the book "Smart Unit Leadership" in the chapter "Skill and Will", you need both. You have to be open to growth and development. Therefore, teach leaders from the beginning that their effectiveness depends on their reception to being taught as well as their natural abilities. You want to make a conscious decision to get better at your craft.

- Communication: this is absolutely the key to good knowledge transfer and is also a huge part of effective leadership. Example: he had a consistent track record of achieving leadership challenges—success. He had a chance to go to survival school which was very demanding; both mentally and physically and changes the way people think and act because it is a high stress environment; very turbulent. Therefore, while in survival school, he decided to modify how he led people to an authoritarian method where he stopped communicating and just told them what to do. This alienated some experienced people who, in reality, wanted to be included. Therefore, this was the worst leadership experience of his career. He failed because he lost the rapport with this team because he had stopped communicating with them, but he learned from this failure. Again, this demonstrates the crucial nature of effective communication.

- The most effective organizations are those that are both task-oriented and people-oriented. The best leaders have these qualities; they work with you; are great mentors who empower their people; make them feel valued, involved, appreciated; recognize their accomplishment towards achievement of the mission and tasks.

References

Armchair General. (2003). Anonymous post, June 4, available at www.armchairgeneral.com/forums/showthread.php?t=12952 (accessed November, 2016).

Biography.com. (N.D.). "Chesley Sullenberger", available at www.biography.com/people/chesley-sullenberger-20851353#crash-on-the-hudson (accessed October, 2016).

Charlier, S. D., Stewart, G. L., Greco, L. M. and Reeves, C. J. (2016). "Emergent leadership in virtual teams: A multilevel investigation of individual communication and team dispersion antecedents." *The Leadership Quarterly*, Vol. 27 No. 5 (2016): 745–764.

Cheong, M., Spain, S. M., Yammarino, F. J. and Yun, S. (2016). "Two Faces of Empowering Leadership: Enabling and Burdening." *The Leadership Quarterly*, Vol. 27 No. 4: 602–616.

Desjardin, T. A. (1995). *Stand Firm Ye Boys from Maine: The 20th Maine and the Gettysburg Campaign*. New York: Oxford University Press.

DuBrin, A. J. (2016). *Leadership: Research, Findings, Practice and Skills* (8th. Ed.). Boston, MA: Cengage Learning.

Dyer, J., Gregersen, H. and Christensen, C. (2009). "The Innovator's DNA." *Harvard Business Review*, Vol. 87 No. 12: 60–67.

Dyer, J., Gregersen, H. and Christensen, C. (2013). *The Innovator's DNA: Mastering the Five Skills of Disruptive Innovators*. Cambridge, MA: Harvard Business Press.

Fawcett, B. (2014). "10 of the Greatest Leadership Mistakes in History", available at www.huffingtonpost.com/bill-fawcett/10-of-the-greatest-leader_b_2057685.html (accessed December, 2016).

Fiedler, F. E. (1967). *A Theory of Leadership Effectiveness*. New York: McGraw-Hill.

Fiedler, F. E. (1981). *Leader Attitudes and Group Effectiveness*. Westport, CT: Greenwood Publishing Group.

Finkelstein, S., Hambrick D. C. and Cannella A. A. (2009). *Strategic Leadership: Theory and Research on Executives, Top Management Teams, and Boards*. New York: Oxford University Press.

Gettysburg (film). (1993). Warner Brothers.

Greenleaf, R. K. and Spears, L. C. (2002). *Servant Leadership: A Journey into the Nature of Legitimate Power and Greatness* (25th Anniversary Edition). New York: Paulist Press.

Hallinan, J. T. (2009). *Why We Make Mistakes: How We Look Without Seeing, Forget Things in Seconds, and Are All Pretty Sure We Are Way Above Average*. New York: Broadway Books.

Hemphill, J. K. (1949). *Situational Factors in Leadership*. Columbus, OH: Ohio State University Bureau of Educational Research.

House, R. J. (1996). "Path-goal theory of leadership: Lessons, legacy, and a reformulated theory." *Leadership Quarterly*, Vol. 7 No. 3: 323–352.

Kahn, J. (2011). "Apple's Investments Outside R&D Spur Innovation", 9to5Mac, available at https://9to5mac.com/2011/10/17/apples-investments-outside-rd-spur-innovation/ (accessed May, 2017).

Kenny, D. A. and Zaccaro, S. J. (1983). "An estimate of variance due to traits in leadership." *Journal of Applied Psychology*, Vol. 68 No. 4: 678–685.

Kickul, J. and Neuman, G. (2000). "Emergence leadership behaviors: The function of personality and cognitive ability in determining teamwork performance and KSAs." *Journal of Business and Psychology*, Vol. 15 No. 1: 27–51.

Kidder, T. (1981). *The Soul of a New Machine*. Boston, MA: Little Brown.

Kouzes, J. M. and Posner, B. Z. (1995). *The Leadership Challenge: How to Keep Getting Extraordinary Things Done in Organizations*. San Francisco, CA: Jossey-Bass.

LaFantasie, G. (2008). "Joshua Chamberlain and the American Dream", in Boritt, G. S., *The Gettysburg Nobody Knows*. Bloomington, IN: Indiana University Press: 31–55.

Longacre, E. G. and Chamberlain, J. (2003). *The Soldier and the Man*. Cambridge, MA: Da Capo Press.

Lord, R. G., De Vader, C. L. and Alliger, G. M. (1986). "A meta-analysis of the relation between personality traits and leader perceptions: An application of validity generalization procedures." *Journal of Applied Psychology*, Vol. 71 No. 3: 402–410.

Maclean, N. (1992). *Young Men and Fire*. Chicago, IL: The University of Chicago Press.

McPherson, J. M. (2003). *Battle Cry of Freedom: The Civil War Era*. New York: Oxford University Press.

Nassar, S., Raja, U., Syed, F., Donia, M. B. L. and Dan, W. (2016). "Perils of being close to a bad leader in a bad environment: Exploring the combined effects of despotic leadership, leader member exchange and perceived organizational politics on behaviors." *The Leadership Quarterly*, Vol. 27 No. 1: 14–33.

Sullenberger, C. B. and Zaslow, J. (2010). *Highest Duty: My Search for What Really Matters*. New York: William Morrow.

Vroom, V. and Yetton, P. (1973). *Leadership and Decision Making*. Pittsburg, PA: University of Pittsburg Press.

Zaccaro, S. J. (2007). "Trait-based perspectives of leadership." *American Psychologist*, Vol. 62 No. 1: 6–16.

4

CULTURE

Leaders need to take ownership of culture. Our primary influence as leaders in business is always on the people.

—Ann Rhodes, People Ink

Corporate culture is the only sustainable competitive advantage that is completely within the control of the entrepreneur.

—David Cummings, Co-Founder, Pardot

It's important for us to create a culture of innovation—one that both values and rewards risk.

—Barbara Landes, CFO, PBS

In this ever-changing society, the most powerful and enduring brands are built from the heart. They are real and sustainable. Their foundations are stronger because they are built with the strength of the human spirit, not an ad campaign. The companies that are lasting are those that are authentic.

—Howard Schultz, CEO, Starbucks

Earlier we talked about leadership and its role in knowledge management and innovation. Leadership is important for the organization and for its continuity over time—but it is insufficient in and of itself in fostering the development of knowledge and innovation. Organizations see leadership transition all the time for a variety of reasons (managers move to another organization, retirement, death, etc.). How then, does an organization preserve the best aspects of itself over time? It is through the establishment of a culture that transcends individual managers and leaders and holds the organization together over time, but changes as necessary as both the competitive environment and the broader organizational context changes over time. Culture is the glue that binds the new employee with existing employees and aids in the continuity of the organization.

Importance of Culture

Why is culture so important? We all know that culture is the shared values and norms that create the bonds that tie us together or the barriers that keep us apart. More specifically, culture has been defined as the set of shared values, attitudes, goals and practices that characterizes an organization. Even though we can define culture, it is still a difficult concept to understand without experiencing it. Very often individuals recognize the culture of their organization when the culture is gone, as often happens in mergers and takeovers. But as might be expected, organizational culture is not the same across geographic borders. You can check your cultural intelligence quotient using Figure 4.1 in this chapter. As organizations become more internationally diverse in terms of employment, sensitivity to different cultures will challenge overall organizational culture.

Think of an organization that you have been associated with for a period of time (so that you have "felt and experienced") and compare that to another organization that you have experienced. Do both organizations have the same "feel", the same values, attitudes, goals and practices? If you have not had such experiences, consider two organizations that you have heard of—the United States Marine Corps and the Walt Disney Corporation. It should not be difficult to recognize that they have two very different cultures. This is an important point to understand, every organization has a culture that reflects the uniqueness of the organization and that fits the needs of the organization. There is no one way, no right or wrong way, to design an organizational culture. But let us be clear, an organization will develop a culture of its own over time, and if no attention is paid to that culture, then it can become a toxic culture and inhibit the ability of an organization to act responsibly and threaten its very survival. A vivid example of culture that was out of control can be found in the collapse of Enron. Enron at one time was one of America's most admired corporations. A company that was widely respected, saw its ethics and culture gradually become corrupted. As a consequence, it went bankrupt and several of its executives went to prison (Johnson, 2003; Fusaro and Miller, 2002). The tragedy here, among many, is that the culture of Enron was not strong enough to survive the manipulations, greed and lack of ethics of the leadership. As such it should be clear that culture and leadership are intimately connected and supportive of each other.

Recently in the U.S. we have been overwhelmed with accusations (and actual guilt) that have swept the media industry. Well-known award-winning actors, producers and directors have been found to be guilty of sexual harassment. In television, numerous famous celebrities have also been caught as perpetrators. It suggests that, at a minimum, there was a culture in these organizations that tolerated sexual harassment and that it was so very strong as to intimidate powerful women into silence. Such is the power of culture.

Culture, according to Osterwalder et al. (2016), can be compared to a garden. As with a garden, you cannot control every aspect, but you can, over time, nurture and care for it. According to them, culture has three components—outcomes, behaviors, and enablers and blockers.

Outcomes and Behaviors

Outcomes are the things that you want your culture to achieve and what you don't want it to foster. The visible parts of an organization's behavior are manifested in the behavior of its employees over time and with each and every interaction with customers and others. Jan Carlzon (1989) noted this in his work, *Moments of Truth.* When he wrote this book, he was the CEO of Scandinavia Airlines (SAS). He argued that each and every interaction that a customer had with a SAS employee (ticket agent, flight attendant, baggage handler, etc.) built the reputation and understanding of the organization—or as the book termed it, a "moment of truth" for the airline. In this book he provides details on how he developed this culture of service amongst his employees and the positive results it yielded. A key ingredient of this culture was affording employees autonomy in dealing with customers. In highly innovative organizations, autonomy and flexibility is crucial to continued successful innovation, and it led to innovation at SAS.

Nordstrom is another corporation that is known for its extraordinary customer service and has maintained that focus for a very long time. One component of this success in customer service is found, according to Tushman and O'Reilly (2002) in the employee handbook that everyone is given upon hire. It states:

WELCOME TO NORDSTROM
We're glad to have you with our company.
Our number one goal is to provide outstanding
customer service.
Set both your personal and professional goals high.
We have great confidence in your ability to achieve them.
Nordstrom Rules:
Rule #1: Use your good judgment in all situations.
There will be no additional rules
Please feel free to ask your department manager,
store manager, or division general manager
any question at any time.

Look closely at Nordstrom's guidance above—it clearly states what the expected behaviors are from their employees and simultaneously allows for discretion in dealing with customers. Note also that the firm has only one rule and that employees are encouraged to seek guidance and ask questions. This approach has led to great innovations in customer service at Nordstrom.

Another method to encourage behaviors and clarify/specify behaviors that are reflected and supported by the culture of the organization is through a process of socialization. The initial process by which employees are hired and brought into the organization (and we will return to socialization later in this work). In World War II, young troops were sent to basic training together and were often put on boats together for the month-long (or more) trip across the Atlantic or Pacific. During this time, they developed strong bonds, and built a "culture". Once in theater, "every harrowing day for a serviceman during World War II was potentially his last. To help bolster troops against the horrors of combat, commanders encouraged them to form tight 'buddy' relationships for emotional support" (Hanson, 2014).

The Navy Corpsman who was embedded with combat Marines in Iraq and Afghanistan told us,

> If the culture is cohesive, the knowledge will be shared more. If the culture is competitive, it will not be shared as much. In combat, the culture is more concerned with the well-being of the group as a whole. Also, the more you share important knowledge and take care of someone, the more they will want to reciprocate. A huge part of the culture of the Marines is to be responsive and adapt, so information/knowledge sharing is critical in doing that. The Army may be more bureaucratic, so knowledge sharing may be more difficult.

In a book by Mark Greenblatt (*Valor: Unsung Heroes from Iraq, Afghanistan, and the Home Front*, 2014), he explored the culture and bonds of U.S. troops fighting in Iraq and Afghanistan. "It is a narrative framed by the warrior ethos: "I will always place the mission first. I will never accept defeat. I will never quit. I will never leave a fallen comrade." "The biggest theme was camaraderie. The Army is like one big family, which always reminds me that I'm not alone in this." "The guys do repetitive deployment because of the brotherhood. They don't want to be away from their buddies. It's a 'brotherly love.' I don't think a lot of people understand the bond that the war-fighters have after combat tours."

The Army Ranger Captain who we interviewed supported this with his story:

> The Company Commander had a policy that the leader was in charge and would have both the responsibility and the authority to order whatever support was needed. This was critical to the success of the mission because in battle, there is no time for requests for permission. In effect, he would become the Company Commander during a battle where he was in charge. They trusted each other and had high standards. You were expected to function as a leader above your pay grade when in danger and you had support from everyone and knew that help was on the way. The Battalion Commander gave people responsibility and authority so that you knew that help would be on the way when you requested it. You had to act very rapidly. Command climate was very important. It's about attitude; you don't know what information will be useful, so take ownership; read and study everything . . . you

(continued)

54 Culture

> *(continued)*
>
> learned to take responsibility for everything. You also learned that praise and credit goes to the platoon and not to you personally; this builds trust and credibility in the unit; it's all about your team. The unit was a family. You had to be disciplined because everyone depended on you with their lives.

Enablers and Blockers

So we develop a culture over time, insure that our employees are socialized into that culture—but how do we enforce the culture over time? According to Osterwalder et al. (2016) it is through the use of formal and informal levers to drive the culture. They saw these "levers" as consisting of four distinct, but nonetheless related, components. The first is easily understood and widely used: incentives. Incentives can be tangible (in the form of bonuses, salary, stock, etc.) or via recognition for good work (in the form of "employee of the month" parking spots for best employees and formal recognition ceremonies). Clearly incentives can enhance the culture of the organization and focus on the positive behaviors desired and not on distracting or negative behaviors.

In addition to incentives, the context and rules signal to employees what behavior is desired and more importantly how those behaviors (and results) are to be achieved. In many fast food restaurants, there are physical timers so that employees can see how long it is taking to serve a takeout customer. The context also provides important cues as to how much flexibility and autonomy employees have in dealing with customers, problems and challenges.

As an example, let's look at Salesforce.com. Their culture deeply values collaboration among many complementary businesses. According to a story in E-Commerce Times,

> Partnering with third parties isn't new for Salesforce.com. A large part of its success can be attributed to the strength of its network of hundreds of AppExchange partners which have either built their applications on Force.com or used APIs and other tools to integrate with Salesforce.com's solutions. Just as the major software vendors of the past built their market shares by encouraging third-party developers to create apps which enhanced their primary products, Salesforce.com has done the same in the even more dynamic world of the cloud. Salesforce.com's partner ecosystem began by appealing to a broad array of start-ups seeking a channel to market for their relatively untested solutions. After gaining a large number of the leading SaaS vendors as AppExchange partners, Salesforce.com set its sights on winning the support of a cross-section of the established ISVs (independent software vendors), major IT consultancies and professional services firms,

as well as an interesting mix of non-traditional software-driven information service providers such as Dun & Bradstreet and Reuters Thomson.

(Kaplan, 2011)

Culture reflects the core values of the organization (if done correctly) and these core values serve as cultural cornerstones. At times these core values can reflect the beliefs and values of the founders—for example the famous "Hewlett Packard Way" (Lencioni, 2002) culture can come to "life" through the use of storytelling. An example was Gino (2015) who recounted that while growing up, he was influenced by a story about how Walt Disney began his career as a cartoonist and commercial artist when he joined the Disney Company. Gino used this story to motivate his own behavior when he was discouraged at work. At Starbucks, employees are told stories about CEO Howard Schultz's great interest in employee welfare. Employees at the Ritz-Carlton Hotel share stories about how employees at every level (cleaning, maintenance, room service) go to great lengths to provide great customer service. The culture can also shape how knowledge is obtained, developed and communicated and lead to improved innovation and overall organizational performance.

The third major component is people. An enduring culture is based on people. The final aspect of culture is, as you might guess, leadership. Starbucks is a coffee shop and bakery that many of us have visited, and it has a very distinctive culture. That culture has been created by years of effort and work. Starbucks sees itself as a provider of an experience not just a seller of coffee, and the CEO of Starbucks has been a consistent figure in the development of and implementation of the firm's culture. It is a place for people to find warmth beyond the workplace and the home. Many training programs in organizations are not just about learning how a firm approaches doing business (e.g., finance of the firm, customer service, emphasis on quality, etc.) but a socialization into the culture, values, goals and expectations the firm has for its employees. At Starbucks, employees are called "partners" (even part-time employees receive stock options and health insurance). In the Starbucks organization, nobody orders anyone to do anything, it is always a request (Leinwand and Davidson, 2016). The core of a working culture and its development is to focus continuously on a few positive aspects, incentivize them and employ good people.

At the end of the day, the culture of your organization communicates your values and what your organization stands for. Do you and your associates want to live and work in a culture of corruption and greed or a culture of innovation, contribution to community and society and making a meaningful difference in the world? What kind of people want to spend a huge portion of their lives in your culture? You need a great culture to attract and keep the best people, and over time the culture becomes so ingrained that it sustains the organization in times of crisis.

Culture has an impact. According to Sørensen (2002) there is extensive research that demonstrates that organizations with strong cultures outperform weak culture firms. Reflecting the work of Osterwalder et al. (2016) a strong culture facilitates consensus and the development of agreed-upon norms of behavior. Strong cultures support and lead to enhanced performance because of reduced uncertainty. Finally, a strong culture improves employee motivation and performance.

Organizational Cultural Types

Cameron and Quinn (2005) have done extensive work on analyzing and categorizing organizational cultural types, as shown in Figure 4.1, in what they have identified as the competing values framework. We believe that these cultural types have significant impacts on knowledge and innovation within an organization.

These four cultures can lead to dramatically different performance levels in the organization and reflect the focus of the organization (inward or out) and how flexible or stable the organization is over time. These frameworks, while useful, are not always definitive of *all of the possible cultural approaches* and organization of culture within the firm. They are a useful rubric for thinking about culture and beginning discussions on culture within an organization or within a specific area of responsibility.

Clan Culture

As one might guess, this organization has a friendly work environment and is very similar to a large, extended family. Employees have a lot in common

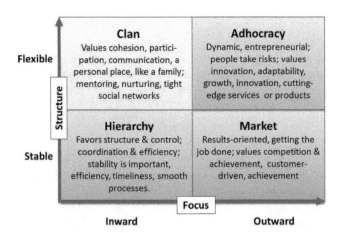

FIGURE 4.1 Cameron and Quinn's Organizational Culture Types (2005)

Source: www.simonassociates.net/wp-content/uploads/2014/01/FlexibilityGraph.png

and the leadership are seen as mentors or as father/mother figures. Loyalty and tradition bind the organization and there is significant involvement by the employees. People are the emphasis and success is measured by addressing the needs of clients/customers. The organization promotes teamwork, participation and consensus. We would speculate that Apple and Google have these types of collaborative, nurturing cultures. Google, for example, is noted for allowing its employees to spend one day a week working on a project of their choice or interest. Obviously Google anticipates that this work will lead to improvement and innovation within Google and potentially new product offerings.

Adhocracy Culture

This is a dynamic and creative working environment. Leaders are seen as innovators and risk-takers and encourage risk-taking by employees. The organization is focused on experiments and innovation. The long-term goal is focused on growth and the creation of new resources. Success is measured by the introduction of new products and services. The organization highly values and promotes individual initiative and freedom. This is an organizational form that celebrates innovation and the development of new knowledge and its application. We suggest that a company like 3M exemplifies this culture with their focus on individual exploration and continual innovation.

Market Culture

Results drive this organization. Emphasis is on finishing work and getting things done. People are extremely competitive and focused on goals. Leaders are hard drivers, producers and rivals at the same time. They are tough and have high expectations. The emphasis on winning binds the organization together. Reputation and success are the most important. Long-term focus is on rival activities and reaching goals. Market penetration and stock appreciation are the definitions of success. Competitive prices and market leadership are important. The organizational focus is laser like is on competition. One of the drawbacks is that knowledge might not be widely shared as that can yield an advantage over others in the organization. As a result, the process and speed by which knowledge is transmitted and shared can be retarded. An example of this culture could be a company like Goldman Sachs that focuses on the bottom line in a competitive environment.

Hierarchy Culture

This is a highly formalized and structured work environment. Rules, policies and procedures drive actions. Leaders are proud of their efficiency-based coordination and organization and functioning smoothly is the most crucial goal. It is the formal rules and policies that bind the organization. The long-term goals are stability

58 Culture

and results, paired with efficient and smooth execution of tasks. Predictability is a highly valued organizational trait. A classic example of this would be the U.S. Army that runs on this hierarchy. In the "old days", most U.S. companies were also based on this hierarchical system, like IBM or General Motors.

As you consider these four types of culture, where is your organization? Where do you want it to be?

Concluding Thoughts

You can create a successful organization by creating a successful culture with these assumptions:

1. Create trust and close relationships if you want to create and share important knowledge. You will not share your most valued secrets with someone you do not trust and respect.
2. Plan and develop deep, on-going socialization experiences continually. This creates richer knowledge transfer but only if the socialization process emphasizes flexibility and the value of innovation.
3. By creating intense socialization, you develop strong ties; strong relationships, a cohesive group, which leads to shared values, mental models, norms, context, meaning, strong relationships and trust.
4. Develop and strongly communicate clear missions, visions and goals. Demonstrate a strong and sincere commitment to your mission, vision and goals; talk is cheap; live your values.
5. Find ways to share knowledge across different groups because bringing diverse opinions and expertise together creates innovation. To do this, you need people who are accepted, trusted and respected in the different groups.
6. Be vigilant in looking for cultural barriers including power and politics. This can destroy an organization when people do not trust each other and can also cause valuable knowledge to be corrupted or just wither on the vine and die.
7. Create a culture of adaptability and innovation. If you can instill a real sense of never-ending curiosity to seek out new knowledge, new processes, new understanding of what your customers want (or what the enemy is doing), new collaborations for continual improvement, then you will always be seeking and achieving innovation. This is in contrast to the old "this is how we have always done it here and we do NOT like change" mentality.

Culture in Practice

1. Uber has been in the news recently, and the news has addressed what many see as a very poor culture. Assume your organization was to be covered in the news with a particular focus on culture—what would that story say?
2. Think about organizations you know and or worked for in the past—what was their culture like? What aspects of that culture did you appreciate?

Culture **59**

3. What are the desired outcomes in your organization? How does the culture support or hinder achievement of those outcomes?
4. What are the desired behaviors in your organization? How does the culture support or hinder performance of those behaviors?
5. How would you go about changing your organization's culture?

Therefore, we recommend that you focus strongly on understanding and possibly changing the culture of your organization if you want to harness important knowledge. Innovation and competitive advantage depend on a culture where people trust and respect each other in terms of strong relationships and competence. In addition, people have to understand each other; creating "shared meaning" where they have the common experiences, language, nuances and insights to correctly understand and learn from each other.

> In World War II, you were part of a family. You took care of each other; you were buddies. The attitudes were different between World War II and Korea . . . "you feel it". You did not have the same closeness in Korea as in World War II. In the Battle of the Bulge, the Ardennes, you had to help each other; like how to keep your feet dry. You had to share these secrets with your buddies or your feet would freeze, get frostbite or gangrene; have to be amputated. You had to change your socks every few hours. You would take the wet socks and keep 4–5 pairs wrapped around your waist to dry them." They all took care of each other.

Before a major battle in Vietnam, our Vietnam Veteran shared some lessons on the culture that helped them survive an ambush. Over half of his recon platoon had been with him for over a year in November 1965 and they felt comfortable and confident with each other. They knew what to expect from each other. He knew them well enough to know what to expect his subordinates to do in the absence of instructions during the battle. Also, everyone was recognized, respected and valued.

> Afghanistan: In combat, the culture is more concerned with the well-being of the group as a whole. Also, the more you share important knowledge and take care of someone, the more they will want to reciprocate. A huge part of the culture of the Marines is to be responsive and adapt, so information/ knowledge sharing is critical in doing that.

60 Culture

Finally, the Army Ranger who was deployed to Afghanistan shared his concluding thoughts on leadership and culture as:

> The most effective organizations are those that are both task-oriented and people-oriented. The best leaders have these qualities; they work with you; are great mentors who empower their people; make them feel valued, involved, appreciated; recognize their accomplishment towards achievement of the mission and tasks.

Veteran Quotes: What Did Our Veterans Have to Say about Culture?

World War II and Korea

- The unit was trained to develop teamwork and take care of each other . . . things like teaching everyone that you had to time the firing of your rifle; like waiting to fire your rifle until your buddy's rifle was empty . . . listen for the "ping" sound and then start to fire your rifle to give him time to reload.
- In his first assignment in the supply division, he found a huge error in an order . . . instead of ordering 2,700 lockers, the order incorrectly stated that they needed 27,000 of them shipped to Europe. Even though he was a young soldier, he had worked with the commanding officer, a Major, for about 4 years and had developed a strong relationship and credibility. Therefore, when he reported this error, the Major believed him. Also, the Major was a good leader; down to earth, cared about his people.
- Credibility is very important in tacit knowledge transfer. Another example of this was when he was in a briefing during WWII about cold weather and how to deal with it. When there were some people in the room who challenged his knowledge, he told them about his experiences fighting in the Battle of the Bulge, the Ardennes, which immediately established his credibility and the knowledge in the briefing.
- Lessons learned in Korea: attitude is important; keep a positive attitude, be flexible/adaptable and be ready for change.

Vietnam

- It makes it easy to lead when the leader and the members of the leader's group know what to expect and feel confident in the leader's decisions and the leader, the group's actions. Over half of his recon platoon had been with him for over a year in November 1965 and felt comfortable and confident with each other. They knew what to expect from each other. A good

Culture **61**

leader must know what to expect his subordinates to do in the absence of instructions. He feels strongly that the success of any organization is based on subordinate. These are the people who are going to make the business successful. The people who work for you need to know and do their job well. He says you must *recognize that everyone is important* and the leader has to *make sure that everyone is recognized and valued.*

- "You knew us, knew our jobs, checked us and that was key to your success." E.g. caring, knowing, learning, admitting mistakes. You see good people, bad people, and you learn from them; continual learning—don't get complacent.

Global War on Terror (GWOT); Iraq

- The Company Commander had a policy that the leader was in charge and would have both the responsibility and the authority to order whatever support was needed. This was critical to the success of the mission because in battle, there is no time for requests for permission. In effect, he would become the Company Commander during a battle where he was in charge. They trusted each other and had high standards. You were expected to function as a leader above your pay grade when in danger and you had support from everyone and knew that help was on the way. The Battalion Commander gave people responsibility and authority so that you knew that help would be on the way when you requested it. You had to act very rapidly. Command climate was very important. It's about attitude; you don't know what information will be useful, so take ownership; read and study everything. This attitude was developed by the Company Commander in military school where you learned to take responsibility for everything. You also learned that praise and credit goes to the platoon and not to you personally; this builds trust and credibility in the unit; it's all about your team.
- The unit was a family. You had to be disciplined because everyone depended on you with their lives.
- This Sergeant was in the infantry. However, he was given an interesting and important position because he communicated with everyone; troops on the ground, headquarters, air support, etc. and acted as a central intelligence hub to keep people safe. He had to learn how to deal with stress and how to communicate information properly; what you say, what you do and who you communicated with were very important. It was also important to learn to get insights from people at all different levels so that you could act as a translator in communicating effectively with everyone in this job; officers and enlisted; to understand and communicate the pieces of the puzzle and get the big picture to communicate the correct information. Because you had to communicate with a lot of different people who had different perspectives and assumptions, you had to learn these. It helped to have worked many different jobs with many different types of people in prior jobs to get a

62 Culture

foundation of knowledge and experience; e.g., gaining different perspectives from prior jobs. Good knowledge transfer mattered because people's lives were at stake and if your communication was not good, they may not have made it home.

- KLE: Key leader engagement. This was a job where he went on missions with officers and met with many different local Iraq leaders of different villages and towns. They would have lunch/dinner with them and ask these leaders what they needed. They would talk about contracts if they needed things like jobs, water systems, etc. These local people were suspicious because their villages had been destroyed and they often had nothing left; no food, water, money, etc. Therefore, the mission was to work with them; to produce "satisfied customers" so that they did not go to the other side for these necessities of life. These local people needed to do what was necessary to feed and clothe their families. Therefore, the mission was to help fill these needs; paid them to do things, set up shops, repaired the water systems, etc. These helped to improve their lives. In this job, he met a lot of different people at each meeting and learned a lot about the different cultures, language; learned to communicate with people from these different cultures and find common ground.
- After Vietnam there was a period of peace time where there was a generation of new officers who had never been in combat. Therefore, there was a disconnect between the combat Veteran leaders from Vietnam and the peace time officers because their experiences were so different and it was difficult for them to communicate because they did not have the same perspectives. After Vietnam there were about two generations of leaders without combat experience so it was difficult to train for the global war on terror. Now you have two generations with war experience who have different cultures, different training, and different perspectives. A business analogy would be if you were looking to hire a new employee. Do you want to hire a young person with no experience but with a college education or someone who comes with a lot of experience?

GWOT; Afghanistan

- Esprit de Corps and comradery are important; people "getting it" for team effort; where people are personally invested.
- Within units, word-of-mouth knowledge sharing is pretty good, especially since it gets spread by people who know each other, have a common background and training, speak the same "language" (acronyms, shared experiences, shared training). Also, as mentioned, people within a unit have developed strong relationships; are good friends and it matters that they share information/knowledge accurately and clearly since they want to take care of each other.

- If the culture is cohesive, the knowledge will be shared more. If the culture is competitive, it will not be shared as much. In combat, the culture is more concerned with the well-being of the group as a whole. Also, the more you share important knowledge and take care of someone, the more they will want to reciprocate. A huge part of the culture of the Marines is to be responsive and adapt, so information/knowledge sharing is critical in doing that. The Army may be more bureaucratic, so knowledge sharing may be more difficult.
- Personalities: There are some "Type A" personalities; people who want power and prestige, but there are also a lot of strong personalities; people who are just as confident and self-assured who can create a collaborative culture and collaborative practices so that information/knowledge can be shared effectively. Sometimes the institution (the team) can make a "Type A" person realize that success comes from collaboration. The overall culture in the Marines supports a collaborative leader.
- Relationships are very important both within and outside the unit. For example, Commander A learns important new knowledge and could call Commander B to share it. However, if Commander A does not like Commander B, then he/she might not make that call to share the new knowledge. But if they like each other, the knowledge will probably be shared. Therefore, good relationships and team building are important.
- This new, innovative Google Earth technique was received in a mixed way, depending on the culture/ organizational climate. Different commanders wanted to see information in ways they were comfortable with. Some commanders only wanted to see the traditional PowerPoint presentations; they were not open to new ideas due to the organizational culture.

References

Cameron, K. S. and Quinn, R. E. (2005). *Diagnosing and Changing Organizational Culture: Based on the Competing Values Framework*. San Francisco, CA: John Wiley & Sons.

Carlzon, J. (1989). *Moments of Truth*. HarperBusiness.

Gino, F. (2015). "The Unexpected Influence of Stories Told at Work." *Harvard Business Review*, available at https://cb.hbsp.harvard.edu/cbmp/content/sample/H02CCT-PDF-ENG (accessed June, 2016).

Greenblatt, M. L. (2014). *Valor: Unsung Heroes from Iraq, Afghanistan, and the Home Front*. Taylor Trade Publishing.

Hanson, D. (2014). "Off Guard: Young World War II Allied soldiers laid bare", Taschen Publishing, available at www.taschen.com/pages/en/catalogue/sex/all/02895/facts. my_buddy_world_war_ii_laid_bare.htm (accessed June, 2016).

Kaplan, J. (2011). "Dreamforce Takeaway: It's All About Cloud Channel Strategies." Ecommerce Times, available at www.ecommercetimes.com/story/73249.html (accessed June 3, 2016).

Leinwand, P. and Davidson, V. (2016). "How Starbucks's Culture Brings Its Strategy to Life." *Harvard Business Review*, available at https://cb.hbsp.harvard.edu/cbmp/content/sample/H03DHC-PDF-ENG (accessed February 3, 2017).

64 Culture

Lencioni, P. M. (2002). "Make your values mean something." *Harvard Business Review*, Vol. 80 No. 7: 113–117.

Osterwalder, A., Pigneur, Y. and Guppta, K. (2016). "Don't Let Your Company Culture Just Happen." *Harvard Business Review*, available at: https://cb.hbsp.harvard.edu/cbmp/content/sample/H02ZIN-PDF-ENG (accessed January, 2017).

Sørensen, Jesper B. (2002). "The strength of corporate culture and the reliability of firm performance." *Administrative Science Quarterly*, Vol. 47 No. 1: 70–91.

Tushman, M. L. and O'Reilly, C. A. (2002). *Winning Through Innovation: A Practical Guide to Leading Organizational Change and Renewal*. Cambridge, MA: Harvard University Press.

5
KNOWLEDGE CORRUPTION

> Knowledge is being aware that fire can burn, wisdom is remembering the blister.
> —*Leo Tolstoy*

> A complacent satisfaction with present knowledge is the chief bar to the pursuit of knowledge.
> —*Jacob Bronowski*

We have been addressing in this work the interrelationships between knowledge, knowledge management and innovation. At the heart of these relationships is the ability to communicate clearly, effectively and accurately across organizational divisions and levels. We know how important accurate knowledge transfer is for the individual and for the organization as a whole—but how do we deal with incomplete knowledge, or knowledge that is corrupted? We again provide examples from our interviews with Veterans that address knowledge corruption at the end of this chapter.

You may be wondering what "knowledge corruption" is. While we have not seen a comprehensive definition of this term in the literature, we view it as information or knowledge that is not correct in some way; whether by accident or by design. This should become abundantly clear in this chapter.

History is replete with famous examples of when knowledge is *not* transferred accurately. Most of you will remember that the explosion of the space shuttle Challenger was caused by a failure of an "O ring" in the shuttle's right solid rocket booster. The vital information did not get to the right people because of fear of going against the power and politics of perceived dominant beliefs and the leadership of the organization. What was most surprising, and mostly under-reported, regarding this tragedy is that the people most affected by the potential

66 Knowledge Corruption

problems with the "O rings" were never informed or consulted. That is, specific information concerning the safety of their rocket ship was not communicated to the crew, which included one non-military member, the first teacher in space. Their lives were the ones at risk, but they were not given a voice in the discussions regarding the safety of the equipment that they were entrusting their lives with in going into outer space. This is, sadly, an excellent example of deliberate knowledge corruption which we will discuss later in this chapter.

The tragedy of 9/11 was replete with poor communications and knowledge transfer problems.

> A new report by the federal commission investigating the September 11 attacks found that rescuers were forced to make rapid-fire, life-and-death decisions based on poor communications, contributing to the World Trade Center death toll. Committee member Sam Casperson, in a minute-by-minute recounting of the second plane's crash into the World Trade Center, detailed how Port Authority workers were advised to wait for assistance on the 64th floor—and many of them died when the tower collapsed. Communications breakdowns also prevented announcements to evacuate from reaching civilians in the building, Casperson said. One survivor of the attacks recounted calling 911 from the 44th floor of the south tower, "only to be placed on hold twice".
>
> *(Roberts, 2004)*

In this chapter, we suggest:

1. Accurate, complete and timely knowledge transfer is critical for organizational or mission success.
2. Knowledge corruption can be caused by several things:

    a. Poor communication processes and practices. In this situation, the communication process itself corrupts the substance and accuracy of the knowledge transfer. It is not deliberate—that is, no individual or group engaged in this corruption—it is the result of communication processes. This results in deterioration of the integrity of the message. Recall the "telephone game" when you were a kid. One person whispered a message to the next person, who whispered it to the next person and so on down the line. By the time the message reaches the last person, "My cat Fluffy loves to eat tuna fish" becomes "The last ant to ruffle the meat became very peckish."

    b. Inadvertent substantive corruption (note all of these can be added to the problem of communication processes) which can be a consequence of, for example, poor training, of individual skills that do not recognize the critical aspects of the knowledge and of other cultural reasons (for example, we do not communicate "bad" news up the line). Here the corruption is a result of organizational norms, culture, past historical practices and approaches to problems and an overreliance on existing explicit knowledge as applicable in all situations and conditions. This would be the example of the "O ring" problem in the Challenger not being communicated to the command center.

c. Deliberately chosen knowledge corruption: a famous example was Pickett's charge in the Civil War when General Lee refused to listen to Longstreet's unusual, strident and consistent assertions that this order would be a suicide mission. In other situations that we have studied (fire-fighters), individuals do not share all of their knowledge with others out of fear of job loss, respect, etc. The problem here is that the corrupted knowledge gets shared with the rest of the organization (or knowledge does not get shared at all) and those on the receiving end believe that they have received accurate knowledge—and they have not. Acting on corrupted knowledge can lead to poor performance and crisis situations.

This only serves to increase the importance of knowledge management, and the ability of organizations to capture tacit knowledge and transfer it rapidly throughout the organization.

The ability to transfer tacit knowledge has been shown as crucial to innovation in organizations and to continual learning and adaptation: both vital in business and military operations. Ledford and Berg (2008) have also noted that tacit knowledge transfer remains elusive in most organizations. General Peter Chiarelli, Vice Chief of Staff for the Army, summed it up nicely: "To stay ahead of our adversaries, we have had to get better at sharing and coordinating knowledge— in order to use it effectively" (Hague and Hoopengardern, 2009, p. 3). However, transferring tacit knowledge is easier said than done, and there is the risk of knowledge being corrupted in the initial stages of knowledge development and in the migration of tacit to explicit knowledge. Abou-Zeid (2004) has argued that there is a significant movement away from viewing knowledge as a commodity and instead looking at knowledge as a process. Some of the major obstacles include geographic distance, inefficient communication processes, knowledge overload (see Hao et al., 2014 and Yang et al., 2014) and, as noted, corruption of the knowledge itself. We also believe that cultural elements, as noted in Chapter 4—such as organizational form, socialization programs (both formal and informal), internal communication processes, power arrangements and politics—and trust and relationships are subtle and critical factors in both the development and transfer of tacit knowledge. Skyrme and Amidon (1997) conducted a survey of more than 400 firms in Europe and North America and concluded that internal cultures are a major, significant barrier to knowledge transfer.

In this chapter, we explore the manner in which knowledge can be corrupted and possible approaches that organizations can take to deal with this challenge. Significant portions of this chapter draw on Jones and Mahon (2012) and Mahon and Jones (2016).

Knowledge Corruption

Figure 5.1 shows a process model of the development of knowledge in an organization as it moves from the tacit stage to the explicit stage. One can note that the very first stage is that the organization recognizes a situation where tacit knowledge might be developed/harvested (recall the example of Wagner Dodge discussed in Chapter 3). Although easily stated, recognizing a "new" knowledge situation is not always as simple as it sounds. If the situation is not recognized, or others do not listen, than no transfer occurs at all. That is, knowledge is not corrupted, it simply is never recognized. It should be evident that in many instances, the ability to recognize a situation where new knowledge has just been developed is severely time constrained—as another new situation is likely to occur in a very short time frame.

If a new knowledge situation is recognized, and the knowledge is captured (as tacit knowledge) it can be transferred, provided that those involved see it as "new" and worth transferring to the rest of the organization. The ability to recognize a new situation can be crucial in communicating the best tacit knowledge, leading to a (hopefully) positive outcome. The ability to "recognize" that a situation or an event or the results of new investigations are "new" knowledge should not be underestimated. If the organization, group, unit or individual does not recognize that they have just discovered new knowledge, no corruption takes place, no transfer takes place, the knowledge simply dies and ceases to exist.

Assuming that "new knowledge" is recognized then a new array of challenges regarding the transfer of that knowledge are possible as shown in Figure 5.2. Note in Figure 5.1 that we recognize the existence of what we term "knowledge hoarding". Knowledge hoarding is the situation where new knowledge is recognized (or discovered) and the individual (or organization) makes a deliberate choice to contain or withhold the information. This occurs frequently in business, in, for example, the pharmaceutical or high-technology industry where advances and discoveries (new knowledge) are held close for competitive reasons. It also occurs in academe, where faculty who have obtained and developed databases do not share them. To be clear, therefore, it must be recognized that new knowledge can be discovered but deliberately not transferred or shared—so this is not a knowledge corruption issue and it is not that new knowledge is lost, it is contained, or hoarded by those that initially possess it.

Note though, that there are four possible paths for tacit knowledge transfer in the organization. The first, and clearly the best alternative, is that the tacit knowledge is transferred accurately and substantively in a timely manner for use throughout the organization. In highly turbulent situations (see Mahon and Jones, 2016), the ability to recognize the new situation and transfer accurate tacit knowledge quickly will theoretically result in the best outcome, especially on the battlefield in highly competitive, rapidly changing environments and in those competitive situations subjected to intense competition and equally rapid changes in the external environment.

Knowledge Corruption 69

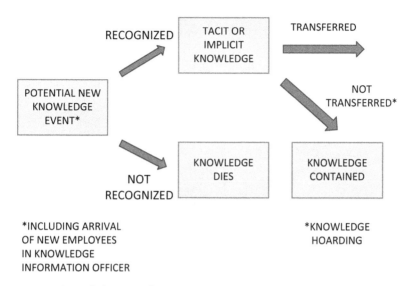

FIGURE 5.1 Knowledge Transfer

But there are three other transfer possibilities—the first is a function of poor communication processes and practices. In this situation, the communication process itself corrupts the substance and accuracy of the knowledge transfer. It is not deliberate—that is, no individual or group engaged in this corruption—it is the result of communication processes. You might recall the frequently used communication exercise noted earlier, where an individual whispers something into a person's ear and they then turn and share that with the person next to them. The last person is then asked to repeat what they were told—and it is often not a match with the original message.

This can, of course, be corrected by greater attention to those processes to insure accuracy and that substantive communications do actually occur. However, there is always a tradeoff in communications between speed and accuracy—again, driven by the contextual environment and the culture of the organization.

The other two forms of corruption are more problematic and difficult to deal with organizationally. Knowledge can be corrupted by inadvertent substantive corruption (note all of these can be added to the problem of communication processes, yielding a situation where all three aspects of knowledge corruption exist simultaneously) which can be a consequence of, for example, poor training, of individual skills that do not recognize the critical aspects of the knowledge and of other cultural reasons (for example, we do not communicate "bad" news up the line). Here the corruption is a result of organizational norms, culture, past historical practices and approaches to problems and an overreliance on existing explicit knowledge as applicable in all situations and conditions. Again, the knowledge corruption here is not deliberate, but a function of the organization's own culture. Although it is not deliberate, it is very difficult to overcome as it is

70 Knowledge Corruption

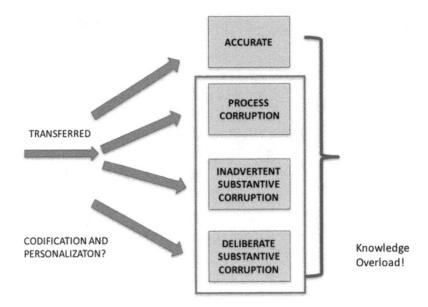

FIGURE 5.2 Knowledge Transfer Options

simply not recognized routinely by individuals or the organization. Defense of the "status quo" is often a barrier to knowledge transfer in organizations.

The last option, however, is deliberately chosen knowledge corruption. We will see that in some situations, military leaders do not transfer substantive knowledge learned as it could be embarrassing to the officers in charge or to the reporting of the overall "success" of the operation. In the Challenger situation that opened this chapter, all the relevant agencies (Morton Thiokol, NASA and others) decided *not* to share the knowledge of the "O rings" with the crew, with disastrous results. In other situations we have explored via intensive interviewing (firefighters), individuals do not share all of their knowledge with others out of fear of job loss, respect, etc. Other examples were provided by the Veterans that we interviewed:

> Knowledge corruption is often personality-driven. Sometimes when someone gets to a position of authority; with the ability to make a difference; 20 years or more; their knowledge may not be relevant anymore. There may be generational gaps which makes it difficult to communicate with younger people. In addition, there is often a top-down approach. For example in the 1990s the officers were peacetime officers and their major focus was on things like accountability of equipment, "Garrison operations", discipline, training management, and uniformity. It was also a very competitive environment. Therefore, in order to advance, officers would take credit for many things and hoard knowledge.

Battle captains in the tactical operations center (TOC) may discount the information coming in which can lead to knowledge corruption, because of their past experience which may cause them to make bad decisions. For example there have been cases where officers have been criticized and not received earned promotions or honors if they have pointed out corrupt knowledge in after-action reviews or other feedback sessions.

"Acceptable risk": some officers will make poor decisions to avoid negative consequences for themselves. Good officers sometimes leave the military because of this corruption.

The problem with corruption of knowledge, no matter what the reason or cause, is that the corrupted knowledge gets shared with the rest of the organization and those on the receiving end believe that they have received accurate knowledge—and they have not. Acting on corrupted knowledge can lead to poor performance and crisis situations.

Finally, there are situations where knowledge is being developed so quickly, and communicated so rapidly, that the recipients of the knowledge are simply overloaded. This is a situation where knowledge can simply be lost—it can be transferred accurately or suffer from the conditions noted, but it gets lost in the sea of communications.

We now turn our attention to other challenges with knowledge transfer beyond the concerns of knowledge corruption.

Knowledge Transfer Challenges

Creating shared meaning to transfer tacit knowledge often requires clear communication (including a common language base and an understandable set of and use of symbols), shared experiences and common backgrounds and cultures. Examples include idioms and prior experiences as necessary conditions for people to both transmit and receive true shared meaning in knowledge transmission.

In addition, the idea of dense networks to share tacit knowledge involves this concept of shared meaning among people who have developed strong relationships, have many commonalities from time together and can share their tacit knowledge relatively easily (for example, through the use of mental models, see Cooke et al., 2000). In contrast, people who are very different, whether they come from different socio-economic or ethnic cultures or have different careers and backgrounds, have greatly increased challenges in sharing tacit knowledge since they lack a common frame of reference with different nuances, language idioms, and perceptions (see Drach-Zahavy and Somech, 2001). This layering of communications of tacit knowledge to include the use of idioms, metaphors, common frames of reference and the like all add to the potential for knowledge corruption. The use of email, for example, has allowed for rapid communications and dissemination of information and knowledge—but emails can be misunderstood and the lack of immediacy (in terms of feedback and ability for on the spot clarity of the communication) is lost.

72 Knowledge Corruption

However, developing social processes that encourage a shift in identity where members see themselves as part of a team encourages cohesiveness and tacit knowledge sharing (Barrett and Snider, 2001; Durden, 2010.) Furthermore, creating social networks of people who can effectively transfer tacit knowledge requires socialization and time working together (Jackson, 2011). Simply put, the development and sharing of tacit knowledge in organizations is either improved by a flexible and constantly evolving culture or inhibited by a culture that is closed to knowledge sharing. However, it should be noted that there can be "too much" of a team orientation that can inhibit the development and sharing of knowledge (Cooke et al., 2000). The aspects of socialization and training that impact and interact with knowledge management and innovation will be explored in more depth in the next chapter.

Perhaps one of the strongest dense groups of networks can be found in the training and socialization of US Marines. During boot camp, recruits go through an intense socialization process that shapes their attitudes and instills a culture that supports the group. This society is rigorous and strict, indoctrinating members that self-discipline, toughness, teamwork, responsibility and accountability as well as a respect for authority are paramount. They learn that in their "warrior society" they must develop the trust and team cohesiveness that will accomplish their mission and get them and their "band of brothers" home alive (Polleck, 2000; Ambrose, 2001). Yet it is this same emphasis on the team or group that can lead to "groupthink" and inhibit the recognition and development of tacit knowledge. Al-Alawi, Al-Marzooqi and Mohammed (2007) in their research found that highly bureaucratic or hierarchical organizations are time consuming and hinder the transfer of knowledge. This is an example of organizational structure encouraging group thinking as well as inhibiting the transfer of knowledge. In our interviews with military Veterans we were surprised by the passionate commitment to the observation that "our training prepares us for everything" and that when asked if they ever encountered a "new situation they were not prepared for", the answer was uniformly no.

In this intense socialization process, Marines learn the values and norms expected in this culture where mission accomplishment and the team are more important than the individual.

However, Marine leaders also stress the welfare of the individual, emphasizing that each person is a vital part of the team. This culture stresses self-actualization with intrinsic motivation to continually perform better, take responsibility and act in a professional manner. Therefore, while Marines collectively strive to support the mission and the team, they also develop unity, cohesion and shared values and norms that allow them to communicate and share tacit knowledge very effectively, if they recognize a new tacit knowledge situation.

There is a loyalty to the Marine Corps and to the individual simultaneously. The individual members trust and respect each other and rely on the predictability of behavior in battlefield situations. In interviews with Marines, it was clear that a fundamental aspect of their training was that they were prepared for

Knowledge Corruption **73**

any eventuality. This framing of preparation can actually inhibit the development of tacit knowledge as no situation is ever seen as "new" or "unique" and therefore the participants may not recognize that they are faced with an opportunity to develop tacit knowledge in new situations. However, active participation in decisions is encouraged in this culture, enhancing the potential quality of the ultimate decision. In addition, the culture also ensures that while subordinates respect the chain of command, leaders also make sure that ideas rise to the top (Durden, 2010; McKittrick, 1984).

In the theory of weak ties, if a person can span different groups (networks) effectively, this person can act as a conduit of tacit knowledge transfer since they can effectively liaise and become an interpreter between disparate groups or networks (this is sometimes referred to as a "boundary-spanner or 'gatekeeper'"—see Morrison (2008), and Morrison and Rabellotti (2009) for a more detailed discussion of knowledge gatekeepers). But this individual must hold a visible position of trust with both groups or networks to be effective in knowledge transfer and serve as a boundary-spanner. The value of this tacit knowledge transfer is the ability to bring new ideas and perspectives into a group to create new knowledge as a result of sharing the tacit knowledge from the other group (Nieves and Osorio, 2013; Murray and Hanlon, 2010).

An interesting example of a boundary-spanner was found in a study of the Australian film industry:

> One of the roles of the producer, a key role, . . . is that the one person who can see the whole picture, with all of the different departments, some cocooned or some interrelating with certain areas, but not with others, and making sure that everybody in fact is working for the same film, but working effectively and coordinating and communicating well with everybody in an area.
>
> *(Alony et al., 2007, p. 49)*

They contend that "'betweeness centrality'—the number of ties one has, connecting otherwise disconnected individuals" (p. 49) determined the effectiveness of their boundary-spanning role between different dense networks.

Creating effective channels for tacit knowledge transfer in distributed environments like multinational corporations (MNCs) or military operations in different towns or countries is very important. Capturing and transferring the local knowledge and know-how from one unit or area to another can be vitally important. Storytelling often represents a very powerful mechanism to transfer tacit knowledge. Stories capture the context as well as create metaphors to transfer knowledge while embedding values and norms. Because stories are often vivid and entertaining, they are memorable and they transfer rich tacit knowledge and experience by creating shared mental models that develop or enhance the absorptive capacity of the participants. While the core tacit

74 Knowledge Corruption

knowledge can be maintained, the stories can be added to over time and vary based on the culture and the recipients. Therefore, a story can be retold in a number of ways so that the different recipients understand the context and the meaning and the knowledge "lessons" of the story remain current. Lambe (2004) explored this further with research that demonstrated using storytelling in the context of cases and games helped to facilitate the transfer of rich, complex, contextualized knowledge among business people. The World Bank has used storytelling and videos to transfer both knowledge and cultural norms to new employees.

Panahi et al. (2012) found that social media can simulate face-to-face tacit knowledge sharing to some extent in the dimensions of social interaction, experience sharing (such as storytelling), observation (often through videos like YouTube), networking and mutual trust.

Furthermore, in turbulent, high velocity environments (Jones and Mahon, 2012), the ability to proactively scan for relevant events in the external environment, share that new tacit knowledge effectively with the people who need it in real time and then to respond effectively to these events in real time becomes crucial. While technologies may be necessary for information flow, the effectiveness of transferring this tacit knowledge is essentially determined by the ability of the sender and receiver to create shared meaning and understanding of this knowledge (Mukherjee, 2007) and this must occur in real time. That is, the "capture" of tacit knowledge must be undertaken shortly after it is recognized and developed or it is lost, or what is "remembered" is not accurate. In addition, sharing tacit knowledge among disparate organizations involves similar factors including long-term relationships between the different organizations with the development of trust and mutual frequent communication (Pak, Ra and Lee, 2015; Nissen et al., 2014; in press). The greater the relationship-strength between and within organizations, the greater the tacit knowledge transfer effectiveness with resulting innovation and performance (Cavusgil et al., 2003). A final challenge in the transfer and sharing of knowledge across organizations is the tension between exchange of knowledge and protection of that knowledge (Yang et al., 2014).

Impact of Culture on Tacit Knowledge Transfer

How does culture impact tacit knowledge transfer? Years of research have revealed some common themes including the importance of trust and developing strong relationships among people to facilitate tacit knowledge sharing.

Rijal (2010) suggests that in turbulent, uncertain environments, organizational culture needs to be flexible and adaptive with a transformational culture that supports innovation, transformation, change and risk-taking. This is in contrast to a transactional culture that is based on the status quo with rigid rules and structures. In his research, he found that especially in rapidly changing, turbulent environments, innovation is crucial to the success of an organization. In addition, Rijal found that leaders in these environments need to communicate a clear and compelling mission and vision to associates while helping them respond to environmental turbulence. He argues that this occurs via innovation and creativity and an environment that embraces a philosophy of continual learning. Similarly, these qualities also include trust, openness and communication. Furthermore, strong bonds of trust in cohesive teams and social networks facilitate this tacit knowledge transfer that gets stronger over time with increasing absorptive capacity of the knowledge base among the team members (Cooke and Lafferty, 1987). However, Jones and Leonard (2009) extend this theory by suggesting that organizations should promote an innovative culture that also is collaborative to respond to turbulent, quickly changing environments.

Dhanaraj et al. (2004) further suggest that the degree of relational embeddedness that results from long-term relationships and trust along with the absorptive capacity of understanding each other over time in these relationships is a significant cultural factor in the effective transfer of tacit knowledge. They further contend that in turbulent environments, relationships and social networks may play a critical role in knowledge transfer. Since tacit knowledge exchange is context-specific and time-bound, long-term relationships with frequent communication that creates the foundation of absorptive capacity and shared understanding facilitates learning and tacit knowledge exchange and by implication, the development of explicit knowledge. It is intuitive that people who have had common experiences will similarly have common understanding and can transfer tacit knowledge more readily.

However, an interesting theory on dimensions of trust from Holste and Fields (2010) suggests an additional layer of complexity in this area. Their research identified two major types of trust: "(1) affect-based trust, which is grounded in mutual care and concern between workers; and (2) cognition-based trust, which is grounded in co-worker reliability and competence" (p. 129). Their research findings showed that both types of trust were necessary for effective tacit knowledge sharing. While caring, concern and a strong relationship (affect-based trust) influenced the willingness to share their tacit knowledge, the competence of the sender (cognition-based trust) was the critical determinant of the willingness of the recipient to use that knowledge. This is a crucial distinction—that one has to be "open" to hearing the tacit knowledge from a specific sender *and* that the competence of that sender is a critical factor in the receiver actually using that knowledge.

Holste and Field's theory is supported by Alony et al.'s (2007) research on credibility or reputation. They suggest that "the effect of network cohesion is by reputation—the existence of more third-party ties around a person promotes sharing information regarding the person and their willingness to assist in the process of knowledge transfer" (p. 50). In their research, they found that inter-connected dense networks resulted in effective tacit knowledge sharing because of the commonality in backgrounds and strong relationships. Similarly, credible boundary-spanning

76 Knowledge Corruption

individuals among these different interconnected networks were able to transfer tacit knowledge because of their reputations in the different groups.

Other researchers have found that collectivist (supportive, constructive) cultures that promote values of trust, encouragement, affiliation, achievement and self-actualization facilitate tacit knowledge sharing more than hierarchical or individualistic cultures. In addition, cultures that focus on shared objectives, empowerment, ownership and solidarity among the team are also more likely to effectively share tacit knowledge because they develop trust among the team members and will share valuable tacit knowledge. Therefore, of the three major types of organizational culture—bureaucratic, innovative and supportive—the supportive culture is seen as being most important in facilitating tacit knowledge sharing. This further infers a team approach where colleagues are seen as strong communities with strong relationships, collaboration, trust, learning and communication (Alavi et al., 2005; Leidner et al., 2006; Girdauskienė and Savanevičienė, 2007; Bajracharya and Masdeu, 2006). Ambrosini and Billsberry (2007) further suggest that organizational fit in terms of culture and values is an additional requirement for effective tacit knowledge transfer. While organizations can work to socialize employees with organizational values and culture to some extent, people who share fundamental values would be more comfortable and likely to create shared meaning in tacit knowledge exchange. Most likely these individuals share symbols and common interpretations of these symbols.

Ipe (2004) found in a qualitative research study that cultural factors including intrinsic feelings of commitment to the goals and mission of the organization as well as feeling valued for tacit knowledge sharing were major motivators in sharing valuable tacit knowledge.

Additional Knowledge Management Challenges

In addition to the potential for corruption of knowledge, there are other aspects that can lead to difficulty in accurate sharing and understanding of "new" knowledge. They include: (1) recipient "blindness", (2) knowledge hoarding, (3) knowledge retention, and (4) knowledge decay and loss over time.

Recipient Blindness

A colleague approaches you with "new knowledge"—how do you, as a receiver of this knowledge, know that it is not corrupted and that it has been transferred accurately? Clearly if you are working closely with this colleague or have the ability to independently verify the knowledge received, there is likely to be no issues of concern. But as distance between units of an organization and individual increase, and the very real pressures for action, it is possible for the recipient to receive, unbeknown to them, corrupted knowledge.

The only solutions that we can offer for this situation is whenever possible to triangulate the knowledge received. In the news business, in theory, stories are not reported unless there are several sources that verify the essential information and story. This may simply not be possible in situation of knowledge transfer.

Knowledge Hoarding

We have noted this earlier—it is the situation where someone or an organization makes the deliberate choice to withhold the transfer of knowledge to others. Simply put, there is nothing that can be done in this situation as others (individuals and the organization itself) may be totally unaware that hoarding has taken place. The knowledge of the problems with the "O rings" known by NASA, by Houston and by Thiokel was "hoarded" as it was not shared with the Challenger crew at any time.

Knowledge Retention

The assumption most hold is that once knowledge is transferred, it is retained . . . but is it? For example, most of us have received initial policy and procedures manuals upon employment and they usually contain an ethics code and other required information. But how many of us can recall that code of ethics on demand or answer other specific questions regarding that knowledge. Organizationally, retention concerns are often a consequence of individuals leaving or retiring. That is, long term employees may unconsciously hoard knowledge—that is their history with the organization has allowed them to develop useful knowledge in the performance of their job. When they leave or retire, they take this knowledge with them and as such it is lost to the organization and to the person who replaced them. This does raise for us the issue of who is in charge of knowledge retention in the organization? We believe that it should be a major focus of Human Resource departments.

Knowledge Decay

The science of Scientometrics studies decay and argues that knowledge, like radioactivity, decays over time. This essentially suggests that once knowledge is developed and transferred, it starts, over time, to decay. As an example consider "mesofacts": these are facts that change very slowly, but we do not recognize it, and we make decisions based on these outdated facts. For example 50% of the existing, explicit knowledge about hepatitis and cirrhosis has been overturned in the last 40 years, yet many physicians are still using the older knowledge. Consider in your organization, who oversees knowledge decay? Who should?

Concluding Remarks

This narrative from an Iraq War Veteran sums up the points we have been trying to address in this chapter:

- In contrast with peacetime officers, the Global War on Terror (GWOT) officers are very different. There has been a change in attitude in the G1 officers to caring more about the lower-level troops. Therefore the war has dramatically changed attitudes and now the lowest-level troops are the most important. The competitive environment in the 90s; peacetime, tended to create some toxic officers. In addition, the generational differences with these officers impeded good communication and knowledge transfer. For example there was an officer who had been from the peacetime era who only knew how to talk to upper-level battalion commanders but did not know how to communicate with lower-level people. There were drastic communication differences between the upper- and lower-level people and therefore the information did not transfer well.
- There are many differences in the skill sets and experiences between the younger and the older soldiers. An average young soldier is often right out of high school with a lower education level. Therefore as an officer you need to know your audience and recognize that there is often a huge variation in your audience so you need to be able to speak the language of each audience and essentially be a translator.

Therefore, what were the lessons learned from these different Veterans? To avoid knowledge corruption, trust and shared meaning are important. When people have very difference experiences and backgrounds, it makes it difficult to understand each other and thus, knowledge can be easily corrupted. Related to the points made in the prior chapter on culture, attitudes are also very important in good communication and knowledge transfer. If people have an attitude or an agenda involving ego, power or politics, or just resistance to change, they may not be willing to listen and will interpret information/knowledge to fit their own mental models. Similarly, if there is a culture of fear, people may simply not share important knowledge. Finally, a bureaucracy may corrupt knowledge when it goes through many channels and gets changed during transmission or, when codified within the bureaucracy, may lose its real meaning.

One method of mitigating these issues is through socialization of new employees to the organization and its cultural norms and through continuous training and education that reinforces those aspects of knowledge management and its transfer that the organization deems to be of importance. We now turn our attention to socialization and training.

Knowledge Corruption in Practice

1. Have you ever been in a situation where a colleague had information and data dealing with an organizational problem that you did not possess? How did you deal with this?
2. Have you ever withheld data, information or knowledge from others? Why? What were the circumstances?
3. How can you insure the accuracy of data and knowledge that you receive?
4. Who is responsible for knowledge "storage" and updating in your organization?
5. Do you have personal examples of knowledge corruption?

Veteran Quotes: What Did We Learn from Our Veterans About Knowledge Corruption?

World War II and Korea

- Credibility is very important in tacit knowledge transfer (to prevent knowledge corruption . . . so that people will listen to what you have to say). When he was in a briefing during World War II about cold weather and how to deal with it, some challenged him, but when he told them his experience of fighting in the Battle of the Bulge, the Ardennes, it established his credibility and they listened to him.
- (This relates to training and communication) . . . Problem with Korea . . . it was difficult when the North Koreans were charging at you; difficult to train people to control emotions . . . e.g. don't fire and empty it until its time and also don't empty the rife too fast . . . it will overheat and you will also run out of ammunition. Therefore, knowledge can be corrupted in a crisis situation when people are reacting emotionally.
- The attitudes were different between World War II and Korea . . . "you feel it". (Again, this infers that knowledge corruption can occur when people communicate, but do not really understand each other; lack of common frame of reference, nuances, etc.)

Vietnam

- Knowledge corruption: a mark of a leader—when you enter an organization, you need to learn as much as possible about that organization and the people who are serving under you. Don't try to make major change immediately; unless it's a crisis. If so, let your experience guide you to do what seems to be correct. (Therefore, developing shared meaning and communication can prevent knowledge corruption.)

80 Knowledge Corruption

- In discussions about the difference between different generations and Veterans or troops in different wars, this retired Sgt. first class mentioned that in World War II the units went over together as a group and often spent months together in training and on the ships in contrast Vietnam Veterans went over as individuals then assigned to unit and then often returned home as an individual. Therefore, the World War II troops were able to develop strong bonds and relationships that the Vietnam Veterans may not have had the opportunity to do.
- Knowledge corruption: you need trust. For example in Vietnam, in a helicopter medevac unit, there were always two people and you had to have a great bond between these people. You would not let anybody fly helicopter that was not safe. Therefore the pilots had to trust the maintenance people that the helicopters were safe to fly.

Global War on Terror (GWOT); Iraq:

- Knowledge corruption is often personality-driven. Sometimes when someone gets to a position of authority; with the ability to make a difference; 20 years or more; their knowledge may not be relevant anymore. There may be generational gaps which makes it difficult to communicate with younger people. In addition, there is often a top-down approach. For example in the 1990s the officers were peacetime officers and their major focus was on things like accountability of equipment, "Garrison operations", discipline, training management, and uniformity. It was also a very competitive environment. Therefore, in order to advance, officers would take credit for many things and hoard knowledge.
- In contrast the GWOT officers are very different. There has been a change in attitude in the G1 officers to caring more about the lower-level troops. Therefore the war has dramatically changed attitudes and now the lowest-level troops are the most important. The competitive environment in the 90s; peacetime, tended to create some toxic officers. In addition, the generational differences with these officers impeded good communication and knowledge transfer. For example there was an officer who had been from the peacetime era who only knew how to talk to upper-level battalion commanders but did not know how to communicate with lower-level people. There were drastic communication differences between the upper- and lower-level people and therefore the information did not transfer well.
- There are many differences in the skill sets and experiences between the younger and the older soldiers. An average young soldier is often right out of high school with a lower education level. Therefore as an officer you need to know your audience and recognize that there is often a huge variation in your audience so you need to be able to speak the language of each audience and essentially be a translator.

Knowledge Corruption **81**

- Enlisted people receive only the information needed. In contrast, officers get way too much information. In contrast to the Army, the Marines are more specialized; their missions are more focused such as a fast strike, but the Army has broader missions. For example Marines will often make the first strike and then the Army can take over and provide a much broader range of services and missions. The Navy also provides support to the Marines for many other operations. Also, the Army is so much bigger. You have to make your mark in the Army; make things different. Most officers want to "shake things up" to make their mark.

- Battle captains in the TOC may discount the information coming in which can lead to knowledge corruption, because of their past experience which may cause them to make bad decisions. For example there have been cases where officers have been criticized and not received earned promotions or honors if they have pointed out corrupt knowledge in after-action reviews or other feedback sessions.

- "Acceptable risk": some officers will make poor decisions to avoid negative consequences for themselves. Good officers sometimes leave the military because of this corruption.

- There are tools and training in place to allow leaders to send/receive information very quickly and precisely without requiring a lot of extra information. This allows us to make critical decisions in a timely manner. However, knowledge corruption can undermine this process resulting in poor decisions.

- When his superior told him that he would have to take over for him he was worried but knew that he had the best knowledge of his unit rather than an infantry person who did not know anything about his unit so he decided that he was the best person to keep his unit going. Therefore his knowledge of his troops and equipment was crucial. Again if they had sent an infantry E7 to take over he would not know how to operate everything. Therefore he prevented knowledge corruption and future problems.

- The infantry guys pushed these concrete barriers using vehicles against his advice. In other words, the infantry people used maintenance equipment that was not adequate to do the job of pushing the concrete blast war walls. The infantry lieutenant ignored and discounted his knowledge which caused the transmissions of the vehicles to break down. There is something of a class war in the Army between the infantry and the maintenance. They always go together but the infantry regards themselves as superior to maintenance. In military culture the infantry is valued more.

- He communicated with everyone; troops on the ground, headquarters, air support, etc. and acted as a central intelligence hub to keep people safe. He had to learn how to deal with stress and how to communicate information properly; what you say, what you do and who you communicated with were very important. It was also important to learn to get insights from people at all

82 Knowledge Corruption

different levels so that you could act as a translator in communicating effectively with everyone in this job; officers and enlisted; to understand and communicate the pieces of the puzzle and get the big picture to communicate the correct information. Because you had to communicate with a lot of different people who had different perspectives and assumptions, you had to learn these.

- After Vietnam there was a period of peace time where there was a generation of new officers who had never been in combat. Therefore, there was a disconnect between the combat Veteran leaders from Vietnam and the peace time officers because their experiences were so different and it was difficult for them to communicate because they did not have the same perspectives. After Vietnam there were about two generations of leaders without combat experience so it was difficult to train for the global war on terror. Now you have two generations with war experience who have different cultures, different training, and different perspectives.

- Knowledge corruption (bad knowledge): for example IEDs changed during the war. However, sometimes old knowledge about the IEDs was used but this old knowledge was not effective against the IEDs anymore. It was difficult to change the minds of the people who were used to the old knowledge; old methods; you needed to repeat the new knowledge to them over and over again that the old methods did not work anymore and there were new dangers to be aware of and different ways to respond to them. Another example was that there were snipers in the city, so you needed to learn how to detect/scan for them. He had to go out and do this to demonstrate to his people the dangers; establish credibility with his unit so that he could translate this new knowledge about the snipers to them so that they would understand and embrace this new knowledge. He also had to get them to understand that the enemy is human, so you can study, learn about them and anticipate what they will do.

- The advisors in the field were the hardest people to teach because they did not have the common training, so they did not have a common core of knowledge or understanding to absorb new knowledge until they had been in the field for awhile. You had to continuously communicate the intelligence. He also learned that a good way to correct bad behaviors was to model the correct behaviors.

GWOT; Afghanistan

- Some of the formal training had the potential to lead to knowledge corruption because of the bureaucracy. When knowledge is codified, it can lose some of the contextual meaning; some of the nuances of the tacit knowledge. Therefore, when knowledge was codified into training manuals, it may have lost some of the real meaning, especially compared to showing someone in the field. In addition, when information is shared and interpreted throughout channels, there is the possibility of knowledge corruption

Knowledge Corruption **83**

when each person interprets it a little differently; similar to the "telephone game" played by kids.

- If the culture is cohesive, the knowledge will be shared more. If the culture is competitive, it will not be shared as much. In combat, the culture is more concerned with the well-being of the group as a whole. Also, the more you share important knowledge and take care of someone, the more they will want to reciprocate. A huge part of the culture of the Marines is to be responsive and adapt, so information/knowledge sharing is critical in doing that. The Army may be more bureaucratic, so knowledge sharing may be more difficult.
- Formalization may also lead to knowledge corruption: people higher up may formulate strategies and when they encounter information from the bottom that does not support their strategies or their information, they may change or suppress that information.
- Knowledge corruption: you have a new set of eyes in a new situation. In unit turnovers, the guys who are leaving are eager to go and the new unit is eager to discuss ideas with them to learn and start working. However the old unit is proud of what they did and sometimes they may come on too strong and turn off the new people in the new unit just arriving. New people have new ideas that they want to test out. A concept known as shadowing helps people transfer this knowledge by conducting actually day-to-day activities and is usually used extensively between units and individuals as they turn over with the incoming counterpart replacing them. The culture should not penalize perceived failures in order to encourage knowledge transfer.
- Example: a sniper is at the front of the line and sees something. When he passes that information back down the line, it is like the telephone game where it gets passed through many people and at the end, often is vastly different (inflated). Therefore, never trust the first report from the end person who received that final information because the knowledge probably did get corrupted. However, in hindsight, if you think about 9/11, perhaps if people had reacted to the final report, the tragedy may not have happened? Therefore, you need to look at the nature of the report and possibly develop a worst case scenario; if we use this information, what could happen and what would it cost?
- Knowledge transfer between venues: you have to be careful about transferring knowledge because the situations can be very different, so the knowledge may not be appropriate or applicable to the new situation. For example, tactics in Iraq might not be relevant in Afghanistan because Iraq was fought in the city and Afghanistan in the rural countryside. However, you may still have some knowledge that you can transfer between different situations. For example, knowledge about IEDs could be transferrable between Iraq and Afghanistan. Therefore, the leadership challenge is to evaluate the knowledge for relevance in different situations.

84 Knowledge Corruption

- Toolkit or kitbag: this is an analogy where you have a duffle bag full of stuff and you need to select the right stuff from the bag that is correct for the situation; it is the same with knowledge.

References

Abou-Zeid, E. (2004). "A knowledge management reference model." *Journal of Knowledge Management*, Vol. 6 No. 5: 486–499.

Al-Alawi, A. I., Al-Marzooqi, N. Y. and Mohammed, Y. F. (2007). "Organizational culture and knowledge sharing: Critical success factors." *Journal of Knowledge Management*, Vol. 11 No. 2: 22–42.

Alavi, M., Kayworth, T. and Leidner, D. (2005). "An empirical examination of the influence of organizational culture on knowledge management practices." *Journal of Management Information Systems*, Vol. 22 No. 3:191–224.

Alony, I., Whymark, G. and Jones, M. (2007). "Sharing tacit knowledge: A case study in the Australian film industry." *Informing Science Journal*, Vol. 10: 41–59.

Ambrose, S. (2001). *Band of Brothers: E Company, 506th Regiment, 101st Airborne from Normandy to Hitler's Eagle's Nest*. New York: Simon & Schuster.

Ambrosini, V. and Billsberry, J. (2007). "Person–Organisation Fit as an Amplifier of Tacit Knowledge", Paper presented at the 1st Global e-Conference on Fit, available at www.fitconference.com.

Bajracharya, P. and Masdeu, N. (2006). "Tacit knowledge transfer in small segment of small enterprises", Master's Thesis in Business Administration Strategy & Culture: Ekonomiska Institutionen Linköpings Universitet.

Barrett, F. and Snider, K. (2001). "Dynamics of Knowledge Transfer in Organizations: Implications for Design of Lessons Learned System." *NPS-GSBPP-01-002*, Naval Postgraduate School: Monterey, California, available at www.dtic.mil/dtic/tr/fulltext/u2/a390917.pdf.

Cavusgil, S., Calantone, R. and Zhao, Y. (2003). "Tacit knowledge transfer and firm innovation capability." *The Journal of Business & Industrial Marketing*, Vol. 18 No. 1: 6–21.

Cooke, R. A. and Lafferty, J. C. (1987). *Organizational Culture Inventory (Form III)*. Plymouth, MI: Human Synergistics.

Cooke, N. J., Salas, E., Cannon-Bowers, J. A. and Stout, R. J. (2000). "Measuring team knowledge." *Human Factors*, Vol. 42 No. 1: 151–73.

Dhanaraj, C., Lyles, M., Steensma, H. and Tihanyi, L. (2004). "Managing tacit and explicit knowledge transfer in IJVs: The role of relational embeddedness and the impact on performance." *Journal of International Business Studies*, Vol. 35: 428–442.

Drach-Zahavy, A. and Somech, A. (2001). "Understanding team innovation: The role of team processes and structures." *Group Dynamics: Theory, Research and Practice*, Vol. 5 No. 2: 111–123.

Durden, J. (2010). "Military Communication: Problems, Precedents and Solutions", available at http://thecrimsonvoid.wordpress.com/2010/08/10/military-communication-problems-precedents-and-solutions/ (accessed August, 2015).

Girdauskienė, L. and Savanevičienė, A. (2007). "Influence of knowledge culture on effective knowledge transfer." *Engineering Economics*, Vol. 4 No. 54: 36–43.

Hague, J. and Hoopengardner, D. (2009). "Knowledge Management in the Department of Defense", paper presented at the ASMC PDI, available at www.slideshare.net/joannhague/kmdodhoopengardnerhague.

Hao, J., Yan, Y., Gong, L., Wang, G. and Lin, J. (2014). "Knowledge map-based method for domain knowledge browsing." *Decision Support Systems*, Vol. 61: 106–114.

Holste, J. and Fields, D. (2010). "Trust and tacit knowledge sharing and use." *Journal of Knowledge Management*, Vol. 14 No. 1: 128–140.

Ipe, M. (2004). "Knowledge Sharing in Organizations: An Analysis of Motivators and Inhibitors", paper presented at the Academy of Human Resource Development International Conference (AHRD), Austin, TX, (Symp. 20-1), available at http://eric.ed.gov/?id=ED492196.

Jackson, D. (2011). "Using Tacit Knowledge for Competitive Advantage: A Study of Sales Team Performance", Indiana University, in partial fulfillment of requirements for the degree of MBA, available at http://opus.ipfw.edu/cgi/viewcontent.cgi?article=1014&context=masters_theses.

Jones, K. and Leonard, L. (2009). "From tacit knowledge to organizational knowledge for successful KM." *Knowledge Management and Organizational Learning, 27 Annals of Information Systems*, Vol. 4: 27–39.

Jones, N. B. and Mahon, J. F. (2012). "Nimble knowledge transfer in high velocity/turbulent environments." *Journal of Knowledge Management*, Vol. 16 No. 5: 774–788.

Lambe, P. (2004). "Practical Techniques for Complex Knowledge Transfer: A Case Study", available at www.greenchameleon.com/thoughtpieces/complex.pdf (accessed October, 2015).

Ledford, B. and Berge, Z. (2008). "A framework for tacit knowledge transfer in a virtual team environment." *Journal of Knowledge Management Practice*, Vol. 9 No. 2, available at www.tlainc.com/articl158.htm (accessed June 2, 2017).

Leidner, D., Alavi, M. and Kayworth, T. (2006). "The role of culture in knowledge management: A case study of two global firms." *International Journal of e-Collaboration*, Vol. 2 No. 1: 17–40.

Mahon, J. F. and Jones, N. B. (2016). "The challenge of knowledge corruption in high velocity, turbulent environments." *Journal of Information and Knowledge Management Systems*, Vol. 46 No. 4: 508–523.

McKittrick, R. (1984). "An Analysis of Organizational Socialization in the Marine Corps", available at www.globalsecurity.org/military/library/report/1984/MRB.htm (accessed June, 2014).

Morrison, A. (2008). "Gatekeepers of knowledge within industrial districts: Who they are, how they interact." *Regional Studies*, Vol. 42 No. 6: 817–835.

Morrison, A. and Rabellotti, R. (2009). "Knowledge and information networks in an Italian wine cluster." *Planning Studies*, Vol. 17 No. 7: 983–1006.

Mukherjee, A. (2007). "The dynamics of organizational culture and knowledge management", Dissertation Proposal: Perdue University, IN.

Murray, A. and Hanlon, P. (2010). "An investigation into the stickiness of tacit knowledge transfer", paper presented at the 13th Annual Conference of the Irish Academy of Management: Cork Institute of Technology.

Nieves, J. and Osorio, J. (2013). "The role of social networks in knowledge creation." *Knowledge Management Research & Practice*, Vol. 11: 62–77.

Nissen, H. A., Evald, M. R. and Clarke, A. H. (2014). "Knowledge sharing in heterogeneous teams through collaboration and cooperation: Exemplified through public-private-innovation partnerships." *Industrial Marketing Management*, Vol. 43 No. 3: 359–534.

Pak, Y. S., Ra, W. and Lee, J. M. (2015). "An integrated multi-stage model of knowledge management in international joint ventures: Identifying a trigger for knowledge exploration and knowledge harvest." *Journal of World Business*, Vol. 50 No. 1: 180–191.

Panahi, S., Watson, J. and Partridge, H. (2012). "Social media and tacit knowledge sharing: Developing a conceptual model." *World Academy of Science, Engineering and Technology*, Vol. 64: 1095–1102.

Polleck, R. (2000). "Becoming a Marine: Re-socialization for a Higher Purpose", available at www.selu.edu/acad_research/programs/writing_center/pick/backissue/volume27/assets/polleck.pdf (accessed May, 2015).

Rijal, S. (2010). "Leadership style and organizational culture in learning organization: A comparative study." *International Journal of Management & Information Systems*, Vol. 14 No. 5: 119–128.

Roberts, J. (2004). "Communication Breakdown on 9/11", CBS News, available at www.cbsnews.com/news/communication-breakdown-on-9-11/ (accessed February, 2017).

Skyrme, D. and Amidon, D. (1997). *Creating the Knowledge-Based Business*. London: Business Intelligence Ltd.

Talwar, R. and Lazarova, I. (N.D.). "Driving Forces - 100 Trends and Developments Shaping the Path to 2025", available at http://thefuturesagency.com/wp-content/uploads/2013/04/Driving-Forces-100-Trends-and-Developments-Shaping-the-Path-to-2025-Master.pdf (accessed February 1, 2017).

Yang, S., Fang, S., Fang, S. and Chou, C. (2014). "Knowledge exchange and knowledge protection in inter-organizational learning: The ambidexterity perspective." *Industrial Marketing Management*, Vol. 43 No. 1: 346–358.

6
TRAINING AND SOCIALIZATION

<blockquote>
Practice is the hardest part of learning, and training is the essence of transformation.
—*Ann Voskamp*

He who conquers himself is the mightiest warrior.
—*Confucius*
</blockquote>

Why should you care about training? "If you look at the organizations who are industry leaders", explains Tracey Maurer, director of new business development at the University of Vermont Center for Leadership and Innovation, "it's not a coincidence that they invest highly in training" (Leavitt, 2014).

> In essence, learning and development is at the core of what high impact performing organizations do, according to Todd Tauber, Vice President, Learning & Development Research, Bersin by Deloitte.

We have observed that in many businesses, new employees are often just given a brief orientation that consists of completing some HR forms, are instructed to read a policy manual, and perhaps requested to attend an introductory talk on the company; its history and culture. Some companies have mandatory online training in areas like safety, sexual harassment in the workplace and similar.

However, this is a far cry from training in the military where everyone in every branch undergoes an intense socialization process and never-ending training and education. As we have stated in prior chapters, this continual training potentially represents the difference between life and death for some people in

88 Training and Socialization

dangerous situations both on the battlefield and in unstable environments where they may be stationed. This never-ending training and education builds what the military calls "muscle memory". In a quote from one of the Vietnam Veterans, he said that when his unit was ambushed by the Vietcong, he used "intuition" to help him guide his troops through this ordeal, saving many of his men. This "intuition" represents the countless hours of accumulated training, education and experience that culminates in the development of deep knowledge and wisdom to make sound decisions, often in crisis situations. You may find his story compelling and you will be able to see the results of intense training in every detail:

Situation: took place during the Vietnam War: November 3–4, 1965. Large units of the North Vietnamese Army (NVA) were in the Central Highlands. His Squadron Commander instructed his units to find the NVA. He was the Recon Platoon Leader and at 6:00 pm he landed his platoon, along with three other recon platoons, deep in a remote forward landing zone (LZ) where the enemy were moving units in from Cambodia. Each platoon set up ambushes away from the LZ. He had a gut feeling that he was among the enemy and that something was different and that something was going to happen that night. This intuition made him follow all training very carefully about setting up the ambushes. He made sure that no one who had a cold, a cough, etc. went on the mission and made sure that everyone had their faces blacked, equipment tied securely so that there would be no rattling or any sounds. All the little things had to be right since he felt that something was going to happen. He set up an ambush about 500 yards from the LZ with 28 men on a trail about 1.5 feet wide and 2 inches deep; surely a people trail. It was dark when they set up, but then the moon came out and they were exposed from above. He was nervous because darkness was his cover. If the enemy climbed trees in the area they would be exposed. After an hour, they heard voices and could smell food. About 45 minutes later, the first of the enemy moved along the trail through his ambush site. After some of enemy had moved past his unit and when the trail in front of him was crowded with a heavy weapons company he sprang a violent ambush. Standard procedure after an ambush, you search for identification and documents. He knew that they must withdraw since he had ambushed a very large unit . . . So he gave the signal to withdraw and assemble. Before they left the LZ, they had organized the LZ in a circle so that each platoon had a piece to defend. IF they returned to the LZ. In about 45 minutes they were attacked by some of the same enemy they had ambushed. At that time, he realized that he should have had them dig fighting positions before leaving the LZ to ambush. The moon was out, it was light and they did not have good cover. His Platoon Sergeant was killed right beside him. Lesson learned: at night every time you fire your weapon the muzzle flashes. The enemy now knows your position. . . . His Platoon

Training and Socialization **89**

> Sergeant had no cover and did not move after firing, a serious mistake. After this happened he admits that had was confused for a few minutes because this was his first major serious enemy encounter. It is certain that they would have been overrun if they had not been reinforced by a US infantry company. Without reinforcements they would have had to escape and evade a very dangerous manoeuvre.
>
> He said his earlier training and experiences were very important to the success of the mission but he learned many new lessons during the long scary night. He lost two guys.
>
> He did an after-action review (AAR) to share his new knowledge with about 20 guys who were involved in the action and to learn from what they saw and experienced.

Thus, training is an area where we have learned valuable lessons from the military. We believe that in most cases, this is the "weakest link in the chain" in business. While most businesses do not encounter these life and death situations, there is huge value in terms of competitive advantage from continually enhancing the knowledge and skills of all people in organizations.

How it works in the military:

1. Boot camp: In the military, training is never-ending. It always starts with boot camp, an intense training and socialization experience which usually lasts 8–10 weeks depending on the service branch. Boot camp is especially important because it develops norms, values and socialization into the unit. The physical and mental challenges as well as the focus on the mission and the team help people develop a focus, a dedication to the team and achieving the mission and a purpose for what they do. This provides meaning and motivation. In the Army, boot camp also helps people develop character, discipline and buy into the core values (BASEOPS):

   a. Loyalty
   b. Duty
   c. Respect
   d. Selfless service
   e. Honor
   f. Integrity
   g. Personal courage

2. After boot camp, people train in classes, in simulations and in exercises. People can select areas of expertise for training such as logistics, field artillery, maintenance, communications, intelligence or computers among many others. The point is that people receive intensive training in their field initially and continually.

A Few Interesting Examples Involving the Green Berets and Special Forces

> Green Berets spend an enormous amount of time training not only in military expertise, but also in foreign languages, and in practicing the art of teaching military skills. This is because they often spend a lot of their time training, advising and assisting foreign forces abroad. Their success depends on their ability to develop relationships with foreign troops, so soldiers must be empathetic and able to work closely with other cultures and nationalities. "As geopolitical situations change over time, it's not uncommon to find a Green Beret who has spent a decade training allied armies in sub-Saharan Africa in French now negotiating with tribal leaders in Afghanistan in Pashto" (Nagy and Moore, 2015). They also constantly cross-train in skills from medical and surgery to technology operations.

The Special Forces' secret to success is similarly intensive preparation and training. In addition to intense physical and psychological training, the Special Forces teams study each area for each mission as thoroughly as any Ph.D. student. They devour every available resource, whether it is open-source or classified assessments of the political situations, demographics, tribal clans, religious issues, and the history of the area, the economy and power dynamics. In addition, they study the natural resources; the terrain, infrastructure, road maps, power grids, and other physical entities such as the buildings, rivers, ponds, walls, etc. From all of this accumulated knowledge, the team then brainstorms, plans, creates possible scenarios and contingencies and essentially they become as prepared as possible before going on a dangerous mission such as the famous Osama Bin Laden raid in Pakistan. This is similar to the story of our Army Ranger Veteran who told us about his focus on intense training before being deployed by reading everything he could find on the area they would be deployed to as well as talking to as many people who had been there, learning from their experiences and developing his own accumulated expertise. In short, he researched, planned, debated and rehearsed in both combat and follow-on operations.

Many of you, in your past experience, may have been involved in a review, in excruciating detail, of an organizational failure. The purpose of such a meeting was to learn from it (perhaps develop new knowledge) and not repeat it again. Consider this, however: have you ever been involved in such a meeting after a terrific success, to consider why your organization was so successful? We would argue that this is yet another example of how new knowledge can be developed—but few organizations have a culture or a socialization/training process that supports such serious introspection.

What About the Marines?

Another intense training and socialization process occurs in the US Marine Corps. During boot camp, recruits go through an intense socialization process that shapes their attitudes and instills a culture that supports the group. This society is rigorous and

Training and Socialization   **91**

strict, indoctrinating members that self-discipline, toughness, teamwork, responsibility and accountability as well as a respect for authority are paramount. They develop a cohesive culture in this "warrior society" with an intense socialization process.

They also learn the values and norms expected in this culture where mission accomplishment and the team are more important than the individual. However, Marine leaders also stress the welfare of the individual, emphasizing that each person is a vital part of the team. This culture stresses self-actualization with intrinsic motivation to continually perform better, take responsibility and act in a professional manner. Therefore, while Marines collectively strive to support the mission and the team, they also develop unity, cohesion and shared values and norms that allow them to communicate and share tacit knowledge very effectively if they recognize a new knowledge situation.

Thus, there is a loyalty to the Marine Corps and to the individual simultaneously. The individual members trust and respect each other and rely on the predictability of behavior in battlefield situations.

How Is This Valuable to Business?

Any company faces changes and challenges from competitors, changing consumer trends, new laws, changes in the economy, etc. We strongly recommend that businesses radically change their assumptions and paradigms about training and adopt more of a military approach to a never-ending thirst for training, education and new knowledge. This requires leaders to devote resources in terms of time and funding for initial "boot camp" style training as well as a well-planned continual training program for all employees.

Some of our Afghanistan combat Veterans shared their insights on training:
    One highly trained Army senior sniper reflected on how to develop tiers of training throughout the organization with this system:

- Training development: there also has to be a development period. For example, he envisioned a system of tiers where:
    - Tier 1 = the most highly trained, the best of the best; like Special Operations. You expect the best performance from them; sub-par performance is not tolerated and those who do not perform are culled out.
    - Tier 2 = intermediate in expertise, motivation, etc.
    - Tier 3 = the new young recruits who have basic skills and entry level training but no experience. These are the people who need rigid training, absolute discipline to teach them the basics to start on their development to gain a foundation of knowledge, training and discipline.

Therefore, there has to be a succession of training and experience to develop the knowledge, the nuances, the insights needed to progress to the higher levels (tiers).

92 Training and Socialization

Shared Meaning and Real Communication

The following narrative (see box) came from a Navy Corpsman embedded with combat Marine units in Afghanistan. He shares the crucial lessons that he learned on the battlefield that intense, never-ending training with repetitions and constant communications with colleagues results in the ability to develop communication for real meaning. It is the ability to filter out "noise" in order to articulate the true meaning and share valuable knowledge so that colleagues can understand immediately and respond effectively. The shared base of knowledge and communication patterns creates something termed "absorptive capacity" which means that each team member has a solid foundation of knowledge in which to understand and create new knowledge for innovation, especially in high stress, turbulent situations.

The Navy Corpsman, embedded with combat Marines in Afghanistan, learned many valuable lessons including:

Sharing important knowledge/information in crisis situations: Repetition is important; simulate high stress situations in a controlled environment many times. If you do this with some people who you will be working with in the field, you learn how to communicate with them and also learn how to streamline the communications so that you know what to communicate; e.g. the most important information. You also learn to become "hardened"; this also comes with experience—the better you are able to cope with a stressful situation and still communicate effectively and accurately (quality of the communication), the better the end result. Time and clarity is of the essence and often emotions take control and you may communicate "noise" instead of crucial information. However, in crisis situations, you need to share the critical information, so you need to learn to reduce the noise (the unnecessary information) and distil the core, important information (sometimes called "muscle memory"). Your training helps you accomplish this in a crisis situation.

This is what helped save lives in combat situations.

What's the takeaway from the hard-earned lessons of our combat Veterans? Training is never-ending, intense and involves communication, discipline, building relationships, developing an inner sense to quickly assimilate the knowledge and experiences learned over time from the training as well as personal experiences in order to innovate and create new knowledge or solve problems successfully. The "muscle memory" that the Veterans discussed represents intense, never-ending training so that you can develop a rich knowledge base to help make good decisions in crisis situations. It led to the "intuition" that several of them described in combat situations where they could react and make good decisions

Training and Socialization **93**

almost instinctively because of the intense training they had received combined with their different combat and non-combat experiences. Another important "lesson learned" from these combat Veterans is that training also involved building *trust* which is earned and develops over time. This continual training develops the relationships so that the quality of knowledge transferred can be communicated clearly and accurately; critical in dynamic, crisis situations.

Most of the Veterans also went through a mix of different types of training to give them different perspectives and skills. For example, one of the Iraq War Veterans received intense training in different weapons, strategy, teamwork, culture and language among others. In addition, the military rotates people every few years so that they have the opportunity to work with different people who have different expertise and experiences as well as different situations. This cross-training accomplishes several things. It simulates mentorships or apprenticeships so that people learn the rich nuances of different skills by working closely with people in different locations and disciplines. It also increases the knowledge base of individuals, providing them with a complex, solid knowledge foundation that allows them to learn more as they progress in their careers and makes them more valuable with their high knowledge levels.

This continual training provides the ability to adapt and create new knowledge in difficult situations. By having a large and diverse base of training and experiences, the combat Veterans were able to see many different perspectives, create new ideas, innovate in their combat situations, and return home with their buddies. Finally, the military instills a sense of urgency to learn as much as possible in order to survive and help your friends also come home safely; you need to always study, learn from others and adapt.

The Veteran who fought in the Battle of the Bulge during World War II as well as in Korea told us:

> He developed intuition from his many battle experiences and training. He had a lot of advanced training from his World War II experiences; much more that the Korean War soldiers. This included expert infantry training, first aid training by surgeons, how to shoot, repair and clean *all* types of weapons. They also had to learn how to drive *all* the vehicles, repair them, drive them through mud without getting stuck. They guys before him told him how to *not* get stuck, "floor it and hang on!", hand-to-hand combat training, bayonet, etc. He knew how to take care of his people when they got blown up; he took care of all of them.

However, the military is not perfect:

An interesting example of needed improvements in training came from the medics in the battlefield. According to a report by the National Defense University Press,

94 Training and Socialization

Today, we know the actions or inactions of the ground medic, flight medic, or junior battalion medical officer can mean the difference between delivering a salvageable casualty or a corpse to the combat hospital. We expect medics to perform life-saving treatment under the most difficult of circumstances, but we invest minimal institutional effort toward training them to a high level or insisting they train alongside physicians and nurses in our fixed military hospitals during peacetime.

(Mabry, 2015, p. 83)

This represents an interesting admission of the need for even more training in the military.

Are Any Businesses Doing a Good Job with Training?

Yes—we did find a few companies who take training seriously with successful results. One good example is the Ritz-Carlton Hotel. According to an article in *Forbes Magazine* (Gallo, 2007), in addition to a culture completely devoted to incredible customer service, they have never-ending training for all associates. "The luxury hotel chain reinforces customer-service values among employees by investing in daily training that revolves around storytelling." All 35,000 associates go through an intense training process which focuses on service, job skills, communication, problem resolution, relationships and more.

After that, every employee participates in a 15 minute "lineup" every day. Each day at every Ritz-Carlton around the world, employees from every department gather for a 15-minute meeting, known as a "lineup", to review guest experiences, resolve issues, and discuss ways to improve service. This never-ending training serves to build morale and motivation as well as exceptional customer service skills and quality for the Ritz-Carlton.

Training can also lead to the development of an innovative culture. Dave Brubeck, an internationally known pianist and leader of a musical group achieved renown with his "Take 5".

Brubeck had expressed disappointment that jazz had lost its edge in 1961. Most jazz at the time was played in four-four time, but "Take 5" moved to five-four time. It is the biggest selling jazz single of all time. But Brubeck went beyond this innovation, and requires anyone joining his group to have a minimum of 5 years classical music training. He considers this important because of the approach he takes in concerts, where a significant portion of the show is musical improvisation.

Sadly, we did not find many other good examples of continual training in business, which points to a great, unfilled gap. Many organizations send employees off to expensive training seminars and opportunities. It is simply not enough to have one or a few individuals "get better, smarter". More progressive organizations require individuals returning from such training to "pass it on" and to share their new skills and knowledge with those who did not attend. Failure to do so is essentially an organizationally approved process of knowledge hoarding.

What Can Our Businesses Learn from This?

Continual training is crucial! Why? It not only educates people and provides valuable skill development and competencies, but it also creates the "muscle memory" needed to think and react quickly and well in crisis situations or, for most businesses, the ability to continually learn, develop and innovate for competitive advantage. If you want your organization to be successful, you must commit a *lot* of resources to continual training including cross training for all associates. Successful organizations like the Ritz-Carlton build in dedicated intense training over specific intervals in employees' careers as well as daily briefing which provide the mechanisms for improvement, learning and sustainable competitive advantage.

Lessons Learned Checklist: What Kind of Training Should You Provide?

If we benchmark against the Ritz-Carlton as a model of excellence in business, as well as using our military examples, we suggest that any organization could benefit from an intense "boot camp" initial training including:

- Communication
- Teamwork, relationship-building
- Mission and vision of the organization
- Core values of the organization
- Conflict/problem resolution and negotiation skills
- Expertise training in their current field along with a dedicated mentor program.

An organization can institutionalize this boot camp (BC). For example, ABC Corps could have 1–2 week boot camps each month with a set number of new employees such as 20 per session. This would be adapted to the size of the organization and the number of new hires over time. Will this be expensive? It definitely will involve a dedicated training budget. If the organization is large and has the resources and space available to have a dedicated center with housing provided, that would increase the enculturation experience. If the organization is smaller, the BC experience can still be accomplished within the 8:00 am–5:00 pm, Monday–Friday, framework with meals as part of the bonding process.

- After BC, an organization should build in scheduled, continual training for all employees. Since many organizations are operating with lean staffs, an emphasis on cross training can also help to improve productivity and provide employees with greater job satisfaction. There are actually many software solutions on the market to track and plan employee training in a strategic way. A software solution like this makes it easier to develop strategic training initiatives.
- Finally, developing a culture where associates are "thirsty" for new knowledge and continual learning creates an environment where people want

96 Training and Socialization

to learn and continue their personal and professional development. They develop a curiosity and desire to learn as much as they can all the time in order to be as prepared as possible, to become valuable members of the team, to develop their own careers and make a significant contribution to achievement of the goals and mission! The culture should also include a focus on collaboration and knowledge sharing to create new knowledge and innovation on a continual basis.

Is it worth the time and expense to do this? Absolutely!

Here are a few examples of companies that did this with some measured results to show the financial impact of the training investment (Freifield, 2013):

1. Best Buy: In 2011, Best Buy decided to develop a comprehensive training and education initiative for its 167,000 employees. In this program, they integrated learning-training directly into each employee's career development path where employees "progress through learning levels that correlate to where they are on their career journey". What is interesting about this program is that training-education is also tied to recognition and rewards in the company where they are given pins to showcase their achievements as well as "points they exchange for products and customized rewards, and pennants for a given department or store to display on their walls as a source of pride". Analogous to the Olympics, employees can achieve bronze status by "completing training modules and exercises that are foundational in content and complexity". They progress to silver status as they develop in their role, completing more advanced modules. Reaching gold status requires employees to begin leading in their role, completing modules that support their ability to bring others in their department along. Finally, platinum status is achieved when employees have successfully prepared for their desired, or aspirational, role (those choosing "mastery" over "mobility" can still attain the platinum level by completing leadership module). Measurement of this initiative shows that it works! "Stores with the highest number of platinum and gold level employees have out-sold stores with the highest number of bronze and silver level employees by a 3:1 ratio. Since the program has launched, Best Buy also has seen exceptional overall company performance improvement in three key metrics: the close rate improved 129 basis points; revenue per transaction increased $3.31; and services and connections sales increased 37 basis points."

Training and Socialization **97**

2. The health care industry has experienced rapid growth with the aging of the population. In 2012, one company, CHG Healthcare Services, developed a structured training program for new employees while continuing training for two years. (N. B. we would recommend never-ending continual training for all employees!). However, they provided new employees with intense training in their disciplines for the first two months followed by coaching and mentoring by leaders and colleagues as well as greater responsibilities for the first two years. This created greater ownership and commitment by the employees as well as greater teamwork, relationship building and knowledge transfer among all of the employees involved. What was the result of this initiative?

   a. In the first six months of 2012, first-year new hires each generated 15 percent more gross margin than in January to December 2011.
   b. In 2012, first-year new hires contributed 35 percent more booked days per month than they did in 2011.
   c. First-year mentees see roughly a 50 percent increase in monthly days booked when compared to another first-year new hire without mentoring. Mentees also see a 23 percent increase in outbound calls.
   d. Second-year new hires also saw a post-mentoring increase (approximately 20 percent) in their own days booked because of the reminder that came with emphasizing the basics to the first-year new hires.

Finally, if we benchmark against best practices in the military, we would propose a model like the one in Figure 6.1.

Lessons Learned

1. Training and education represent a vital, never-ending process to instil the values, attitudes and knowledge needed to make your business competitive and create never-ending innovation.
2. Top management should incorporate training and education into the strategic plan in order to devote the necessary resources and manage it effectively.
3. Create and nourish a culture that makes learning an integral part of everyone's mission including their performance appraisals. Create an urgency and a thirst for knowledge that will allow everyone to collaborate and share knowledge for sustainable, continual innovation leading to competitive advantage.
4. Build trust and develop strong relationships as part of the training so that people continue to share knowledge for continual innovation regardless of their position or location.

And Now for a Little Theory

Professional socialization has been defined as:

> the process by which an individual acquires the values, expected behaviors, and social knowledge needed to assume an active role in a given profession. The socialization process is part of professional education and leads to the acquisition of symbolic, intellectual, and, to an extent, social capital.
>
> *(Ryazanova and McNamara, 2016)*

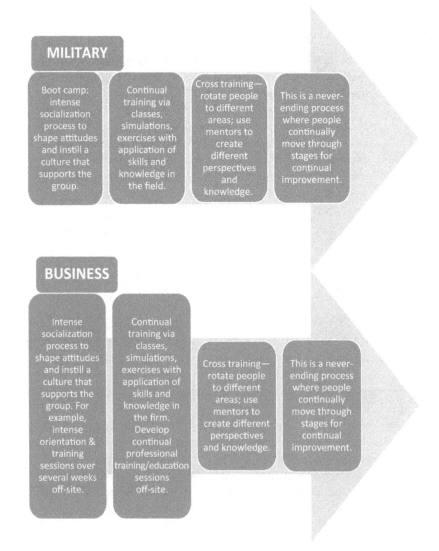

FIGURE 6.1 Learning from the Military—Continual Training Model

These authors further suggest that increased social capital in terms of an extensive network leads to increased collaboration and productivity. We speculate that this would also lead to increased innovation since people who are socialized with shared norms and values would communicate and collaborate more effectively, share knowledge and generate new knowledge.

In another interesting study by Cable et al. (2013), they explored a new view of organizational socialization that focused on the needs of both the individuals and the organization. They suggest that optimal socialization and enculturation occur when the organization recognized and values each person's social identity: a

> person's best self as the "individual's cognitive representation of the qualities and characteristics the individual displays when at his or her best." An individual's best self emerges from using and being recognized for his or her signature strengths, which increases his or her feelings of authenticity.

Therefore, to be successful in the socialization process, an organization should make an effort to accept each person's individual unique perspectives and strengths and attempt to integrate those into the culture rather than "force-feeding" the norms and values to these new associates. This is an interesting contrast with the U.S. Marine Corps which uses the boot camp experience to break down each person's social system and re-acculturate them into the Marine Corps model. Is one approach better or more successful than the other? In traditional socialization theory, researchers have found that when people enter a new organization, the experience creates anxiety, which increases their susceptibility to influence. In addition, there are institutional socialization tactics that can re-acculturate people to the norms and values of their new organization. For example, early and continued training and reinforcement of the accepted norms, values and behaviors can shape and change people's perceptions of "this is how we do things here" and socialize them over time. They usually develop attitudes and values that are consistent with the organization so that they feel part of the team. You often see this when people talk about their organizations as "we do this and we believe that". This is strengthened with mentors and role models who consistently demonstrate the desired behaviors. However, in their research, these authors found that productivity was enhanced when the organization made an effort to recognize and value the unique perspectives and strengths that each person brought into the organization; their personal identity. This is actually consistent with the socialization and acculturation process in the U.S. Marine Corps. Even though they create a strong, unified culture via the boot camp experience, they also value and recognize each person's strengths and contributions to achievement of the task and mission.

The next chapter, 'Knowledge Structure and Processes', explores the possible infrastructures that organizations can use to facilitate effective knowledge transfer. An analogy would be the Internet. There is a huge volume of data and programs that

100 Training and Socialization

we rely on to make our businesses operate efficiently and make our lives easier and more productive. However, without the "infrastructure"—the "pipes" that carry the data in an organized way with efficient processes and protocols—this would not happen. Thus, in the next chapter, we explore the knowledge transfer structures and processes that similarly help organizations and facilitate innovation.

Training and Socialization in Practice

1. What is the on-going process for training in your organization? Does it apply to all employees (regardless of position, gender or age)?
2. Consider how you can use training and socialization as an on-going source of innovation for your firm.
3. When was the last time you underwent training in your organization?
4. Training should not be optional, it should be viewed as not only a reward for past performance but a clear opportunity to develop and grow as an individual manager.
5. Consider unusual training opportunities—one corporation we know in Boston affords employees fully paid training for self-improvement (including retreats, yoga, etc.).

Veteran Quotes: Veterans' Perspectives on Training and Socialization—What Did Our Veterans Tell Us?

World War II and Korea

- The Marine Corps creates a level playing field, which reduces class and status. This was where this Veteran really learned perseverance, fitness and to do things right the first time and every time.
- Problem with Korea . . . it was difficult when the North Koreans were charging at you; difficult to train people to control emotions . . . e.g. don't fire and empty it until it's time and also don't empty the rifle too fast . . . it will overheat and you will also run out of ammunition.
- As a helicopter pilot in Korea, he walked away from three helicopter crashes. Training was the key to the many problems with the helicopters.

Vietnam

- Intuition was something that he used a lot in crisis situations. What is this? A foundation of knowledge to draw upon; develop ability to detect nuances from a lot of training, education, experiences, AARs (after-action reviews).
- He said his earlier training and experiences were very important to the success of the mission but he learned many new lessons during the long scary night. He lost two guys. He did an AAR to share his new knowledge with

about twenty guys who were involved in the action and to learn from what they saw and experienced.

- Difference he sees between military and civilian leadership: Military is not afraid to train their subordinates to become better. Civilian world—more concerned about keeping job and not so apt to train subordinates . . . different incentives.

Global War on Terror (GWOT); Iraq

- He had a lot of training but when he encountered things not learned in training he improvised. People who had been in Desert Storm gained a lot of experience about Iraq and he was able to talk to some of them and learn about the country and culture. For example, an older Master Sergeant told them to expect SCUD missiles and just to take cover.
- It helped to have worked many different jobs with many different types of people in prior jobs to get a foundation of knowledge and experience; e.g., gaining different perspectives from prior jobs. Good knowledge transfer mattered because people's lives were at stake and if your communication was not good, they may not have made it home.
- After active duty, he went into the reserves and taught at West Point. He instructed young cadets using his experiences as a combat Veteran to help them understand. He would "throw out the book" and share his stories and experiences; why you would do certain things. It helped these young students learn more because they were real experiences and he would care more about their lives because he had just gone through it and wanted them to understand so that they could adapt better also.
- In combat, you are under intense pressure and use "muscle memory" from your prior intense training. However, in these liaison, economic missions, learning these new cultures made a big difference. For example you learn from the experiences; different cultures, different perspectives and you develop the ability to translate; communicate effectively among different people.
- In addition to the normal training, he put himself out there to gain information; he gained knowledge over time to develop this intuition. The most decisive point is the point of danger, so you gain this intuition and you develop a "sixth sense" so that when the decision-maker is at the point of attack, you are able to make decisions rapidly; to prevent casualties. You develop the ability to anticipate and detect danger.
- He was an ROTC instructor for several years. At one point, he had an intensive two-day training session with ruthless drills and training to try to perfect their skills. He would study their progress and would teach them from his war experiences with stories from the battlefield like ambushes or searching the enemy while they were still alive to make sure that they did not use their weapons. Also, he would make the point at the end that every bit of effort to prepare for combat is useful since you do not know what you will encounter. You develop your instincts and the amount of effort you put in leads to better instincts.

102 Training and Socialization

- He studied the fire fights, talked to other platoon leaders. Also the Company Commander had a policy that the leader was in charge and would have both the responsibility and the authority to order whatever support was needed. This was critical to the success of the mission because in battle, there is no time for requests for permission. In effect, he would become the Company Commander during a battle where he was in charge. They trusted each other and had high standards. You were expected to function as a leader above your pay grade when in danger and you had support from everyone and knew that help was on the way. The Battalion Commander gave people responsibility and authority so that you knew that help would be on the way when you requested it. You had to act very rapidly. Command climate was very important. It's about attitude; you don't know what information will be useful, so take ownership; read and study everything.
- There are some things you can learn in school, but a lot happens in the field; mentorship and experience.
- Wars are different. In Iraq, it was in the city, so you had to act fast. In Afghanistan, it is out in the country, so the situations may be different; more measured or slower. Therefore, you need to always study, learn from others, and adapt.
- Match the correct type of training with the appropriate audience: A new way of training is called "outcomes-based training"; you create a problem and let a lower-level person without "spoon-fed" training try to solve the problem, and rather than train to an end state, you simply watch them and see how they do in solving the problem. The history of this is that it was originally developed by Special Forces who operate in small environments. An example of this now would be a reconnaissance course, where there was no checking in on the progress. However, the people wanted to get feedback. Therefore, this new approach does not seem to work well depending on the instructor's skills. Theoretically officers want to teach the younger troops how to think vs. what to think. However, telling them what to do helps with control when operating in chaotic situations.
- Good knowledge transfer: The Army has preplanning sessions; they get together with people who are experienced and get tips and insights from them. For example, don't get on the radio unless it is critical because it will jam up the airwaves so the people who need information can't get it.
- Organized chaos: Teach young people to think under pressure and work under chaos. An example is a SALUTE acronym that is taught; where they learn to assess information under conditions of high stress/turbulent environments.
  - o S: Size and/or strength of the enemy
  - o A: Actions or activity of the enemy
  - o L: Location of the enemy and direction of movement
  - o U: Unit identification. The designation of the enemy unit may be derived from unit markings, uniforms worn, or thorough information provided by enemy prisoners
  - o T: Time and date the enemy was observed
  - o E: Equipment and weapons observed

- You never have all the information. Also, you need to teach people to wait and assess. The most important weapon that you have is your radio; to communicate. Therefore, in crisis situations, the training for these salute reports is huge. Everyone knows the acronym and it is crucially helpful in a crisis battlefield situation.
- The advisors in the field were the hardest people to teach because they did not have the common training, so they did not have a common core of knowledge or understanding to absorb new knowledge until they had been in the field for a while. You had to continuously communicate the intelligence. He also learned that a good way to correct bad behaviors was to model the correct behaviors.

GWOT; Afghanistan

- Training development: There also has to be a development period. For example, he envisions a system of tiers where:
    - Tier 1 = the most highly trained, the best of the best; like Special Operations. You expect the best performance from them; sub-par performance is not tolerated and those who do not perform are culled out.
    - Tier 2 = intermediate in expertise, motivation, etc.
    - Tier 3 = the new young recruits who have basic skills and entry level training but no experience. These are the people who need rigid training, absolute discipline to teach them the basics to start on their development to gain a foundation of knowledge, training and discipline.

    Therefore, there has to be a succession of training and experience to develop the knowledge, the nuances, the insights needed to progress to the higher levels (tiers).
- Sharing important knowledge/information in crisis situations: Repetition is important; simulate high stress situations in a controlled environment many times. If you do this with some people who you will be working with in the field, you learn how to communicate with them and also learn how to streamline the communications so that you know what to communicate; e.g. the most important information. You also learn to become "hardened"; this also comes with experience—the better you are able to cope with a stressful situation and still communicate effectively and accurately (quality of the communication), the better the end result. Time and clarity is of the essence and often emotions take control and you may communicate "noise" instead of crucial information. However, in crisis situations, you need to share the critical information, so you need to learn to reduce the noise (the unnecessary information) and distill the core, important information: (sometimes called "muscle memory"). Your training helps you accomplish this in a crisis situation.
- The way you process information; such as assessing a patient who is hurt, communicating to the radio operator and other people what they need to do is critical. You need to analyze the situation, distill what is important, communicate

104 Training and Socialization

effectively the most critical information with short, quick communication to the people in order of priority, so that they can do what needs to be done; help an injured person, get air or ground support, etc.

- Rehearsals (training) help at the beginning. They are run by people who have prior experience in these things. Towards the end of his deployment, he was running these training programs to train less experienced Corpsmen. He had the credibility and the experience so that the less experienced people trusted him and felt more comfortable since they knew he had real, important experience that they needed to learn in order to help others in those crisis situations.
- After every mission, there was a "hot wash" debriefing where the unit would go over what had happened; what went well, what did not, what could have been done better or better ways to do things. For example, they may have noticed that the enemy was doing things differently.
- In addition to word-of-mouth, there were "hip pocket" classes; informal classes in the field or at home. These classes were to share information that was not in the training manuals; things that were new and emerging and important for people to know. If you had a spare hour or two, you would do one of these quick training classes to fill knowledge gaps.

References

Cable, D. M., Gino, F. and Staats, B. R. (2013). "Breaking them in or eliciting their best? Reframing socialization around newcomers' authentic self-expression." *Administrative Science Quarterly*, Vol. 58 No. 1: 1–36.

Freifield, L. (2013). "2013 Best Practices and Outstanding Training Initiatives"; available at www.trainingmag.com/content/2013-best-practices-and-outstanding-training-initiatives (accessed March 16, 2016).

Gallo, C. (2007). "How Ritz-Carlton Maintains Its Mystique", available at www. bloomberg.com/bw/stories/2007-02-13/how-ritz-carlton-maintains-its-mystique-businessweek-business-news-stock-market-and-financial-advice (accessed March 24, 2016).

Leavitt, R. (2014). "How Top Companies Make the ROI Case for Employee Training", SkilledUp, available at https://learncore.com/top-companies-make-roi-case-employee-training/ (accessed September 1, 2017).

Mabry, R. (2015). "Challenges to Improving Combat Casualty Survivability on the Battlefield", available at http://ndupress.ndu.edu/Portals/68/Documents/jfq/jfq-76/jfq-75_78-84_Mabry.pdf (accessed June 15, 2016).

Nagy, C. and Moore, B. (2015). "The Green Berets' Elite Military Training Is the Perfect Preparation for a CEO", available at https://qz.com/401616/the-green-berets-elite-military-training-is-the-perfect-preparation-for-a-ceo/ (accessed June 12, 2016).

Ryazanova, O. and McNamara, P. (2016). "Socialization and proactive behavior: Multilevel exploration of research productivity drivers in U.S. business schools." *Academy of Management Learning & Education*, Vol. 15 No. 3: 525–548.

7

KNOWLEDGE STRUCTURE AND PROCESSES

> In vain have you acquired knowledge if you have not imparted it to others.
>
> —*Deuteronomy Rabbah*

In the previous chapter, we stressed the importance of never-ending training and education to continually increase everyone's base of knowledge and develop a perpetual thirst for new knowledge. As discussed, a rising tide of increased knowledge will benefit everyone and the organization as people share and leverage this new knowledge for continual innovation and sustained competitive advantage.

Why is it now necessary to focus on building knowledge structures and processes? "Build it and they will come" (*Field of Dreams*, 1989) may have worked in a movie, but in real life, you need to proactively set up structures that make it easy and seamless to capture important knowledge as well as to access it and share it easily and effectively.

As mentioned in an earlier chapter, we attributed a poorly functioning culture to inhibiting knowledge sharing and thus, to the space shuttle Challenger disaster with the "O ring" failure. However, we speculate that it was also a failure in not having a good knowledge transmission structure. We know that some engineers knew about the "O ring" problem, so why was that crucial information *not* sent to the people making the launch decisions? We speculate that there was no easy mechanism for the engineers to submit their knowledge about this problem to a system that would be easily available for the decision makers to see. If we could go back in time and change things, we might recommend a "problems portal" that engineers could use to submit important information that was available and necessary for the decision makers to see. For example, a simple knowledge portal could look something like Figure 7.1 for NASA.

FIGURE 7.1 Knowledge Portal Model

The intent behind this portal would be a space where engineers, researchers, decision-makers and others could easily submit information and knowledge that they deemed important enough to share. The "O ring" issue of course would have been submitted into the "Launch problems" space and anything submitted there would be considered extremely important and checked continuously. The ongoing processes section and new technology developments would be organized either by project or by research area to make it easy to submit and to search. The training section would be a place where the processes and new developments could be captured on video or other media to codify and share tacit knowledge more easily. Using emerging AI (artificial intelligence), it would also be feasible for a system to learn about problems, issues and proactively send alerts when it sensed something important that should be shared.

How Has the Military Developed Knowledge Structures and Processes?

Because valuable, recent knowledge can mean the difference between life and death in the military, they have developed good structures and processes to capture and share this valuable knowledge. The U.S. Marine Corps does a great job with this and represents a gold standard for benchmarking.

- After each mission, they do a "hot wash"; also known as a debriefing or after-action review (AAR). The people involved get together as soon as possible while their memories and perspectives are still fresh and share their experiences during the mission; what happened, what they learned, what was new or different, lessons learned. Sometimes it is recorded by someone in the unit; sometimes an intelligence officer will be present to record the information and new knowledge.

- Sharing knowledge: The knowledge recorded from these debriefings are entered into databases such as the "Marine Corps Center for Lessons Learned". A few quotes from the Marine Corps Center for Lessons Learned include:

  o "The Marine Corps Center for Lessons Learned (MCCLL) actively collects, analyzes, publishes and archives lessons learned materials to include observations, insights, lessons (OILs), trends, AARs and Marine Corps lessons learned reports. These efforts support training and planning for both exercises and operations, and the warfighting capability development process. MCCLL focuses on tactics, techniques and procedures of immediate importance to the operating forces thereby identifying gaps and best practices, and recommending solutions across the doctrine, organization, training, materiel, leadership, personnel, and facilities (DOTMLPF) spectrum."
  o "All DCs, Directors, and Commanders compile and submit lessons learned to the Marine Corps Center for Lessons Learned."
  o "Amid the high risk and uncertainty of combat, shared experience-especially lessons hard-earned should be promulgated laterally as quickly as possible so that the learning curve of the entire organization is elevated by the creativity or misfortune of the individual units."
  o "We will apply lessons learned from current operations to maintain an edge against ever-adapting opponents."

- There is a well-documented and applied process whereby people in each unit are designated to record these after-action reviews to capture knowledge.
- They send their reports up the chain of command where subject matter experts review the knowledge content to filter for the most important knowledge.
- This knowledge is then entered into specific databases and shared in training exercises, classes and other knowledge sharing activities.

Thus, they have both formal and informal channels to share knowledge. The informal channels work well if you have a direct relationship or have regular direct contact. For example, after a mission, you can talk with others in your unit who you trust and respect. However, if you attempt to share some new knowledge with people outside your unit who do not know you, they would have to know whether to trust your knowledge; you would not have the required credibility to share tacit knowledge easily. Thus, by establishing more formal mechanisms to share valuable knowledge and integrate some vetting mechanisms to build trust in the system and the knowledge, it can potentially be shared more readily.

108 Knowledge Structure and Processes

An interesting story about Marines using after-action reviews shows the value of developing structure in knowledge acquisition and knowledge creation.

In 2005, during the intense offensive in Iraq, Sgt. Earl Catagnus Jr. and his team of snipers with the 3rd Battalion, 5th Marines "saw street-level action daily, clearing hundreds of houses throughout the city. Each night, Catagnus, 26, and three of his Marines spent a lot of time talking about the lessons from each day; what was working for small units and what wasn't." They were able to document valuable knowledge that they learned and capture it for future teams. For example, they found "Insurgents' escape routes are pre-planned and well-rehearsed through back alleys and rooftops. Marines quickly learned to isolate city blocks after making contact; otherwise, insurgents' escape was certain. Leathernecks learned to use tanks and combined-arms tactics to root out die-hards, being mindful never to put a Marine where you can put a bullet. Using the buddy system and establishing footholds as rallying points also became important in preventing Marines from getting trapped or left behind in houses." They were also able to provide "in-depth descriptions of the urban terrain in Fallujah, a city described unlike any Marines have trained for. From the random, un-zoned layout of the city to the floor plans of a typical house and the number of locks on exterior doors, the report details how Marines improvised to deal with the unfamiliar environment" (Yon, undated).

This type of systematic capture of new knowledge is crucial for survival in the life and death situations faced in the military. For example, another Marine recorded some tactics used by the enemy which illustrates why new knowledge needs to be captured and shared effectively.

The platoon manoeuvred two HMMWVs to the west in order to establish a support by fire position. The enemy ambushed this element with RPG and machinegun fire. They suppressed the turret gunners with their PK machineguns and fired volleys of RPGs at the hood of one of the vehicles. The hood caught fire from the RPG blasts which in turn ignited the rest of the HMMWV. The enemy waited for the crew to dismount and then engaged the dismounts with heavy grazing fire from the PK machineguns. The enemy who attacked the vehicles were within range of the dismounts from the initial ambush but did not participate. The enemy is familiar with our tactics and knew that we would attempt to establish a support by fire position. This is not the only engagement where the enemy has demonstrated an advanced understanding of our tactics (Yon, undated).

Knowledge Structure and Processes **109**

What can we learn from this? In the chapter on training and socialization, we stress that continual training and a culture that promoted an intense desire for continuous learning is crucial for success. That is not enough. You have to develop structures and processes to capture this new knowledge and share it so that the next unit can learn from it. As shown above, by capturing and sharing crucial knowledge, the Marines would have known what to expect the next time and could have been more prepared for a ruthless enemy.

Here is one more excellent example from one of our Afghanistan Veterans:

> Debriefings occur after every mission where people speak freely about the experience and report any new things that may have happened. For example, the team may have discovered that the enemy had been observing their operations and adapting the timing of the IEDs to the protocols of the military known as TTPs (Tactics, Techniques and Procedures). This new knowledge would then be recorded and passed up the chain to the highest level. Ideally, there would be intelligence people at the different levels to review and filter these reports; especially new knowledge so that they could pass important new knowledge up the command so that it would be disseminated throughout the units to teams who were currently operating in the field/battlefield. In addition, the new and important knowledge would be incorporated into the more formalized training sessions that occur for each rank and specialty skills schools. These training sessions occur on a continual basis so that people in different units and different locations can learn what is happening and gain access to the new knowledge that they may need to incorporate when they are on a mission. These training sessions would be heavily rely on the recent after-action reviews (AARs) and lessons learned from previous units operating in a similar or the same environment.

What About Business?

A good example in the business sector in capturing and developing effective knowledge processes would be something like TurboTax. Each year, the complex and dreaded tax return laws change. Given the complexity of the U.S. tax code, most people do not have the knowledge or expertise to complete their taxes correctly unless they have the simplest tax status. Therefore, the experts at TurboTax study the changing regulations and incorporate the new laws and formulas into the software. They use a simple interface with questions and "if-then" processes to guide people on preparing their taxes correctly. For example, TurboTax helps people understand the new Affordable Care Act (ACA) with possible penalties and exemptions. A tax software like this automates the process, integrating their accumulated knowledge of tax law with updated state tax, marriage, health care, business and other constantly evolving tax laws into the program.

110 Knowledge Structure and Processes

Here is another example of developing good knowledge structures and processes in business.

The American Productivity & Quality Center surveyed 84 organizations "to understand the extent to which they have embedded knowledge sharing and collaboration in key business processes and workflows" (APQC, 2011). They found that over half of these organizations, many of which were knowledge-intensive, embedded knowledge in an enterprise-wide integration. The others embedded knowledge processes in unit or functional areas. To integrate valuable knowledge with critical business processes and workflows, they used workflow management software, collaboration technologies and other technologies with the inference being intelligent database solutions (Bullen, 2014; APQC, 2011).

Taxonomies and Ontologies

While these terms are not terribly interesting, they are important to understand if you want to easily capture, harness and share valuable knowledge. First, what do these words mean? Taxonomy is basically the science of classification. How do we group things into logical categories? Ontologies take this a step further and explain why different things are grouped together- how are they similar and why? On the Web, taxonomies and ontologies describe different things to make it easier to search for them, which is the reason why they are so valuable for knowledge management systems and structures.

> For example, suppose several different Web sites contain medical information or provide medical e-commerce services. If these Web sites share and publish the same underlying ontology of the terms they all use, then computer agents can extract and aggregate information from these different sites.
>
> *(Noy and McGuinness, 2000)*

Therefore, when setting up structures to embed valuable knowledge in different processes, it is important to take the time to think about and categorize the knowledge in a way that makes sense to the different people who will need to use it. By describing each type of knowledge in some depth (creating the ontologies), it will make it easier to search and find the knowledge that you need. We have all experienced searching for knowledge that we desperately need for a project, to solve a problem, or to make a decision, only to have search results that are basically garbage and no help at all! This will help to solve this important aspect of effective knowledge transmission.

Here are some examples of taxonomies:

Figure 7.2 shows an example of a classic type of taxonomy about the animal kingdom.

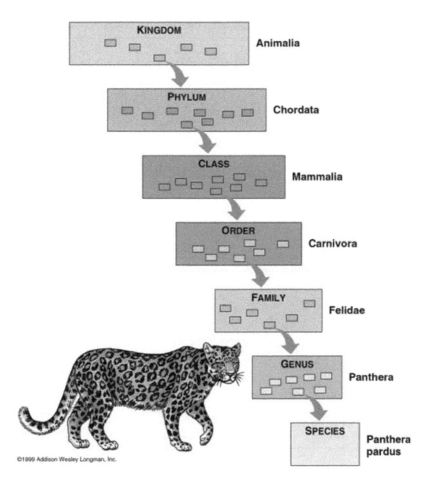

FIGURE 7.2 Example of a Taxonomy
Source: www.mun.ca/biology/scarr/KPCOFGS.html

Therefore, you can see how these are classified and categorized.

Here is another example that deals with a knowledge-intensive research project called Undiscovered Maine (see Table 7.1). In their website map, they show how they are organized and their levels of information in the regions and hidden gems categories. For example, if you needed information or knowledge about what to see and do in western Maine, it would be contained in that section.

112 Knowledge Structure and Processes

TABLE 7.1 Example of a Tourism Business Taxonomy in the Form of a Site Map

Undiscovered Maine	Regions	Hidden Gems	Business

About Us
Our Blog
Contact Us
	Aroostook County
	
	• Caribou
	• Easton/Fort Fairfield
	• Fort Kent
	• Houlton
	• Madawaska
	• Presque Isle
	
	DownEast
	
	• Eastport
	• Lubec
	• Machias
	
	Lakes & Mountains
	
	• Bethel
	• Farmington
	• Jackman
	• Carrabassett
	• Valley
	• Rangeley
	• Stratton
		Activities
		
		• Beaches
		• Biking
		• Boating
		• Breweries
		• Farms
		• Fishing
		• Golf
		• Hiking
		• Historic
		• Rainy Day
		• Shopping
		• Skiing
		• Wildlife
		
		Dining
		
		• By Town
		• Lodging
		• By Town
		• Shops and
		  Services
		
		By Town
		Itineraries
		
		• By Region
			Maine Businesses &
			  Products
			For Entrepreneurs
			Web Creation
			Social Media
			Information Systems

Note: Data from www.mbs.maine.edu/undiscoveredmaine

One last example would be the website map from a knowledge-intensive marketing agency (see Table 7.2).

This shows their areas of expertise—where the knowledge in the company lies. Thus, the concept remains the same: in order to find knowledge quickly and easily, you have to create a structure—a taxonomy to show how and where it is categorized.

An ontology takes this one step further by adding meaning to the taxonomy as well as the relationships between the entities. Therefore, if you are trying to solve a problem and need the great knowledge of an expert, by having an ontology available, you can essentially ask a question about the problem and the information and context within the ontology will allow the (intelligent) search engine to more easily understand what you are really looking for and to help you find that valuable, needed information or knowledge quickly and easily. Figure 7.3 shows an example of an ontology to make this clearer.

TABLE 7.2 Example of a Marketing Agency Taxonomy in the Form of a Site Map

Pulse Marketing	Services	Pulse Academy	Portfolio
About Us • Our Approach • Our Community • Our Team Blog Careers Contact Site Map	• Branding • Content Writing • Email Marketing • Graphic Design • Inbound Marketing • Market Research • Marketing Strategy • Mobile Marketing • Public Relations • Search Engine Optimization • Search Marketing • Social Media Marketing • Traditional Advertising • Video Production • Website Design	• Marketing Blog • Training & Resources	• Email Marketing Samples • Logo Design Samples • Market Research Samples • Print Samples • Search Marketing Samples • SEO Report Samples • Social Media Samples • Video & Audio Samples • Website Samples

Note: Data from https://pulsemarketingagency.com

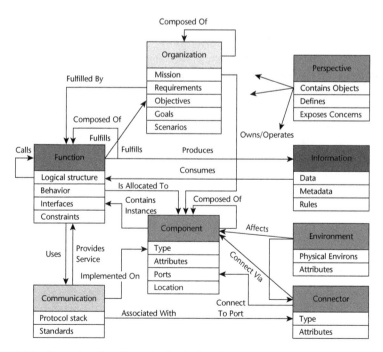

FIGURE 7.3 Example of an Organization's Ontology

Source: https://commons.wikimedia.org/wiki/File:MBED_Top_Level_Ontology.jpg

114 Knowledge Structure and Processes

Lessons Learned: What Can You Take from This to Help Your Business?

- Educate your employees about knowledge creation and knowledge sharing. Many people will not even recognize when they create new knowledge. This goes back to your continual training.
- If someone learns something new, create an easy way to capture that. You can create an easy-to-use knowledge portal as shown with the NASA example at the beginning of this chapter where employees can submit new knowledge or problems. We recommend tying this in with an incentive and reward system to encourage this behavior.
- Along with the continual training, there are other mechanisms like the daily meetings at each Ritz-Carlton where employees are encouraged and possibly rewarded for sharing new knowledge or problems. This will create the important AAR process. Be sure to develop roles and responsibilities for recording and submitting this knowledge to the appropriate databases— knowledge portals.
- Develop a structured process of mentoring where knowledgeable, experienced employees can share the valuable lessons learned with others. Consider investing in the expertise to create a good taxonomy and ontology for your knowledge repository.
- Look into using artificial intelligence (AI) to enhance your ability to develop relationships among the information and knowledge in order to search and find valuable knowledge more quickly.
- Develop institutionalized processes for sharing valuable knowledge and information such as newsletters, announcements and alerts, small and large meetings and events.
- Develop the equivalent of the tactical operations center where new knowledge is sent, reviewed and categorized for sharing as well as a "white paper" or "lessons learned" repository to make knowledge well categorized and easily accessible.
- Develop a communications structure and process with available technologies including telephone, email, social media, texting and other available forms of communication. Train and educate employees on who to communicate with for different purposes; understand the roles and responsibilities for effective networking and communication so that important information can be shared effectively.
- Take the time to think about the knowledge that you need in different departments and throughout the organization to make good decisions, to solve problems, to continually innovate. Then, create categories (taxonomies) and describe them well (ontologies) so that people who need that information and knowledge can actually find it easily.
- Invest in a knowledge librarian to accomplish the points mentioned above.

Knowledge Structure and Processes **115**

And, now for a little theory:

Dynamic capabilities. It is intuitive that if organizations do not respond effectively and quickly to changes in the environment, they are likely to lose market share to competitors who do adapt quickly and often will go out of business. A few researchers have studied this.

According to Teece et al. (2016), all organizations deal with risk and uncertainties. The most problematic is when organizations are faced with unknown unknowns. An interesting quote by Janeway (2012) exemplifies this: "The innovation economy . . . is saturated in unquantifiable uncertainty." If you think about this, the global economy is becoming exponentially more complex as digital systems increase the speed of change and innovation. Therefore, by extension, managing change and uncertainty becomes similarly more complex and challenging. They suggest that developing "organizational agility" represents a smart way to continually and proactively assess and respond to dynamic, turbulent environments. They define organizational agility as "the capacity of an organization to efficiently and effectively redeploy/redirect its resources to value creating and value protecting (and capturing) higher-yield activities as internal and external circumstances warrant" (p. 17). They further detail this in organizational clusters:

1. identification, development, co-development, and assessment of technological opportunities (and threats) in relationship to customer needs (the "sensing" of unknown futures)
2. mobilization of resources to address needs and opportunities and capture value from doing so ("seizing")
3. continued renewal ("transforming" or "shifting").

(p. 18)

How can organizations develop a useful structure to continually and systematically assess and capture changing environments in order to provide agility and ultimately continual innovation? They first make a distinction between processes and capabilities. Processes tend to be slow and difficult to change. While organizations must have good, efficient processes to get the daily tasks done, they cannot stop there. Organization should also look at capabilities which involve having a dynamic culture. Referring back to Chapter 4: Culture, remember that an innovative organization has a culture of continual learning, absorptive capacities, and leaders who embrace change, communication and collaboration as well as autonomy and flexibility. Remember that culture is the glue that binds people together and defines the core values that everyone adheres to. Therefore, leadership that develops a culture of innovation, collaboration, continual assessment and learning is a necessary capability for an innovative agile organization.

Another capability that involves the organizational structure is creating an institutionalized structure that can do the following:

116 Knowledge Structure and Processes

- "Listen"—what they call "generative-sensing capabilities"—(p. 21); capture new knowledge and sense changing conditions.
- Share that knowledge effectively to people in the organization who can benefit from it.
- Facilitate communication and collaboration among people in the organization so that they can work together to create new knowledge for innovation. This also infers the ability to find and harness expertise throughout the organization to combine capabilities for unique new knowledge; innovation.
- Build some flexibility or "slack" into the organization to allow for unexpected changes and the ability to respond and adapt quickly.
- Decentralize the organizational structure to remove rigid hierarchies so that people have the autonomy and flexibility to respond rapidly to changes in the environment and communicate easily with others to adapt, respond and create new knowledge.

This concept of sensing/adapting organizations was further explored by Felin and Powell (2016) that focuses on organizational design, which they suggest is a "crucial enabler of dynamic capabilities" (p. 79). They similarly define the "dynamic capabilities view of competitive advantage" as "success in volatile industries requires higher-order capabilities that enable companies to anticipate, shape, and adapt to shifting competitive landscapes". They also recognize that the traditional hierarchical organizational structure inhibited knowledge creation and innovation. Instead, they suggest that better organizational designs (structures) include "a unique blend of polyarchy, social proofs, self-organizing teams, and open organization—to release the creative power of teams and individuals" (p. 79).

How does this work? These researchers looked at the degree of responsiveness to the environment within an organization as well as how well the organization was able to integrate people to sense, process, share knowledge, collaborate and innovate. Not surprisingly, they suggest that the best organization for continual innovation is one that is highly integrated and has a high capability for sensing and responding to the environment. Their recommendation for an organizational design and structure that recommends "polyarchy" suggests that power is distributed throughout the organization, essentially creating a flatter, more organic organizational structure. This give some degree of power and autonomy to people who are on the "front lines", who are "closest to the action". It also infers that these people will have the capability to communicate and collaborate with others to affect change via a relatively transparent communications structure. This is enhanced by a culture that supports sensing at the front lines and the ability to act upon recognition of changes and opportunities in the environment. For example, if a front-line employee at a hotel paid careful attention to customer questions and requests, they could recognize an unfilled need for something like a mobile app to check in and check out, order room service, concierge service, etc. They would also have the autonomy and communication structure to send this idea to the new product development department for consideration, possibly request participation on the development team, and even get rewarded and recognized for this contribution to the overall mission and goals of the organization by both leadership and their peers.

They integrate this decentralization with a concept called "social proof" that "is any mechanism of social influence that tends to produce coordinated behavior among individuals. The nature of social proofs is to induce a kind of social contagion in which beliefs, preferences, and practices disseminate through a population of individuals" (p. 85). This acts as a self-regulating mechanism where colleagues communicate their observations, ideas, and suggestions to form a "collective wisdom" that will monitor and moderate individual ideas. This is similar to a concept discussed previously in this book, "creative abrasion" (Leonard-Barton, 1995), where people with different perspectives come together to share ideas, provide different alternatives and ultimately create new knowledge and innovation that is usually more creative and more reasonable because of the diversity of perspectives.

Another interesting organizational design that they suggest is something they call "collaborative innovation". In this model, they suggest that an organization create organizational structures to proactively monitor and request feedback and ideas from many different channels including customers, suppliers and other stakeholders who again, have different perspectives and different ideas. With continually emerging new digital platforms such as evolving social media platforms, this becomes easier, especially when integrated with software that can search through many different digital areas, collect and analyze this information, often through artificial intelligence software. Some organizations proactively harness and leverage the ideas from stakeholders via incentives and engage them into the knowledge creation process via focus groups, software testing, or collaborations with suppliers. They suggest that in an increasingly connected world, this opens up many new opportunities for collaboration, new knowledge creation, and continual innovation and competitive advantage.

Furthermore, O'Reilly and Tushman (2013) suggest that organizational ambidexterity—"the ability to simultaneously pursue both incremental and discontinuous innovation . . . from hosting multiple contradictory structures, processes, and cultures within the same firm" (p. 324)—is necessary for the survival of an organization. The term "ambidextrous" infers the ability to do several things well simultaneously. This research model is similar to the prior one by Teece in suggesting that organizations need to develop efficiencies in their stable operations, but they also need to be proactive in sensing and developing new innovative capabilities. In essence, they find a balance between efficiency and innovation. These authors provide a plethora of research to show a positive correlation between organizational ambidexterity and firm growth, financial performance and increased competitiveness. They also found that organizational ambidexterity is more successful in uncertain environments rather than stable ones.

118 Knowledge Structure and Processes

Interestingly, they found that culture plays a huge role in the ability of a firm to be successful at both efficiency and innovation. This reminds us of our example of 3M Corporation in Chapter 2. Their organization culture of continual leaning, collaboration and innovation is supposed by a structure that provides dedicate time for this exploration and collaboration. This is also consistent with the theory of dynamic capabilities in a firm's ability to sense and adapt resources to changing conditions.

Knowledge structure and processes in practice:

1. One of the challenges in knowledge structure and processes is the failure to recognize that:

   a. Individuals learn at different rates
   b. Individuals learn via different modalities (some prefer models, other written instructions and others hands on involvement)
   c. Failure to consider (a) and (b) above results in both individual non-responsiveness and organizational frustration and simple decisions that training is "not worth the effort."

2. Consider offering training opportunities that are unusual in nature, that allow for personal in addition to professional development.
3. It is not enough that one person learns, so consider having individuals who do attend seminars or training opportunities share their new knowledge via a short presentation to others or via direct mentoring of others.

Now that you have thought about the infrastructure and processes that facilitate knowledge transfer, what are some of the important technologies that you can use to actually management and transfer the valuable knowledge? In the next chapter, we will take a look at some crucial technologies that can help your organization capture and share valuable knowledge easily.

Veteran Quotes: Veteran's Perspectives on Knowledge Structure and Processes

Global War on Terror (GWOT); Iraq

- Another important concept is something called TOC which stands for tactical operations center. In this TOC, there is often a battalion commander, radio people, and many other experts needed for the battle situation. When action happens, reports are radioed in to the TOC. The TOC gets reports from all units so that they can get a consolidated picture and knowledge of what is happening as well as intelligence reports, aircraft intelligence, and other crucial knowledge and information that comes into the center. They also act as a way to connect people who need specialized communication with the people who have that knowledge. For example if there is a unit under attack the TOC can connect them directly with the aircraft such as attack helicopters to provide immediate knowledge and communication for the support needed. People on the ground are sending in information and the TOC can control this information and make vital decisions in high velocity/turbulent environments.

GWOT; Afghanistan

- Knowledge transfer: knowledge transfer in small group settings: this is usually how new knowledge is tested out; in the small unit. In the Marines, every unit has a similar structure and a similar mission by category (e.g. infantry, logistics, air, etc.).
- If something works, you can write an (standard operating procedure) SOP, but to share it more broadly, you have to go through formal channels. Example: there was something called "amphibious doctrine" in World War II which was developed by officers at Quantico, during the interwar years, to teach them how to attack a hostile beachhead in the Pacific theater. An officer, Major Pete Ellis, created this valuable new knowledge that was so important that it was disseminated to every Marine in training. This was done between World War I and World War II.
- Marines are considered professionals. There is a publication called the Marine Corps Gazette which is the professional magazine of the Marines where any idea, theory, etc. can potentially be published. Anyone can write and submit something to the editor. The editors will review the submission to possibly publish this content.
- "Point papers": these are papers that codify lessons learned in the field. There is also something called "professional military education" or PME for short. Every rank goes to a PME school for their rank. For example a Cpl. will go to a PME school for that rank to develop them as professionals and leaders. Point papers are taught in those schools. Someone can write a point paper and submit it to their boss who will review it and send it up the chain of command. However there is a newer method now where anyone can submit an idea or "lessons learned" to something called the "Marine Corps Center for Lessons Learned" website (www.tecom.marines. mil/Units/Directorates/MCCLL). Each unit has an operations officer that will usually submit these "lessons learned" after the AAR or point papers on the Marine Corps website. However you need an account to submit lessons learned via this website.
- In addition to the professional military education classes, knowledge is also transmitted by email to people who need to learn that new information. In the field, the communication system uses radios and a system called a Blue Force Tracker (BFT) which allows communication via a texting format in

120 Knowledge Structure and Processes

many cases. There is a term called COC which stands for command operation center. This is a command center where there are people with needed expertise in different disciplines such as an intelligence officer, an analyst, a medical person, an air person, operations officer and so on so that you have hopefully all the needed experience and knowledge in one room to support you when you are out in the field. You are constantly updating the COC in the field via your BFT and radio. There's something called a TO/E or a "table of organization and equipment" which lists all the weapons and equipment each Marine is required to have per job title or billet. All officers are issued weapons, but the true weapon of an officer is his/her radio; not their rifle because knowledge and communication is vital to you being able to operate effectively and control/command their troops in the field or battle.

- When units transition, the departing unit will always spend time debriefing the new, arriving unit with what they have learned throughout their tour. In addition, they will have time for new people to shadow the existing unit before they depart so that they can share their new knowledge. For example, when going on a patrol, the current unit will show the new people which parts of the landscape to look at as indicators of IEDs or good spots for the bad guys to hide and conduct ambushes, etc. After the knowledge is shared, it will depend on the leadership and culture of the new unit on whether and how much of that knowledge they will choose to use or whether they prefer to do things their own way. But most units heavily rely on the lessons learned from the previous unit to continue with the successes already gained by their actions in that area.

- You need to understand the communication structure so that the most important information gets sent up the chain to the people who need it the most: such as air support, supervisors, command center, etc. and also send important information down the chain to people who need it such as medical, infantry, etc. Therefore, training and structure are very important. Training in communication, the hierarchy and how information flows most effectively and efficiently to accomplish the mission are very important. Do you know who to communicate information to?

Tacit Knowledge Transfer

Within the Unit

- AARs (after-action reviews) have been used successfully throughout his career. Ranger school focused on leadership; after every patrol, even at night, you talked about what you did wrong or right and what you will change before the next mission, which might happen in 10 minutes. The AAR was done and then on to the next mission.

- Pay attention to the AAR discussions; take notes and then encourage people to take action of the one thing that was most important. This takes you from intellectual knowledge to action knowledge. He developed a modified AAR process; instead of the normal three good and three bad things normally asked at the AARs, he found that this was too much and it was better to concentrate on the one or two things that you consider most important and that you will use and do better next time. This approach seemed to work better.

Outside the Unit

- He had the chance to work both at the tactical (lower) level and also at the operational (mid) level. The Army likes to create a chain of command process. Therefore, if someone in Company A sees a trend, then they can push that knowledge to Battalion headquarters, who can then push it down to other units. However, Battalion is often so overwhelmed with so much information that sometimes valuable information/knowledge may be lost.

References

APQC. (2011). "Knowledge Sharing in the Flow: Survey Results: How Organizations Are Integrating KM in to Critical Business Processes and Workflows", available at www.apqc.org/sites/default/files/files/Knowledge%20Sharing%20in%20the%20 Flow%20Survey%20Results%20on%20KM%20implementation(2).pdf (accessed March 15, 2016).

Bullen, D. (2014). "How Top Companies Make the ROI Case for Employee Training", available at www.skilledup.com/insights/how-top-companies-make-the-roi-case-for-employee-training (accessed March 15, 2016).

Felin, T. and Powell, T. C. (2016). "Designing organizations for dynamic capabilities." *California Management Review*, Vol. 58 No. 4: 78–96

Field of Dreams (film). (1989). Universal Pictures.

Janeway, W. (2012). *Doing Capitalism in the Innovation Economy*. Cambridge, UK: Cambridge University Press.

Leonard-Barton, D. (1995). *Wellsprings of Knowledge: Building and Sustaining the Sources of Innovation*. Cambridge, MA: Harvard Business School Press.

Noy, N. F. and McGuinness, D. L. (2000). "Ontology Development 101: A Guide to Creating Your First Ontology", available at http://protege.stanford.edu/publications/ontology_development/ontology101-noy-mcguinness.html (accessed March 15, 2016).

O'Reilly III, C. A. and Tushman, M. L. (2013). "Organizational ambidexterity: Past, present and future." *Academy of Management Perspectives*, Vol. 27 No. 4: 324–338.

Teece, D., Peteraf, M. and Leih, S. (2016). "Dynamic capabilities and organizational agility: Risk, uncertainty, and strategy in the innovation economy." *California Management Review*, Vol. 58 No. 4: 13–35.

Yon, M. (N.D.). "The Eagle Went over the Mountain", available at www.michaelyon-online.com/the-eagle-went-over-the-mountain.htm (accessed Jan 3, 2016).

8
TECHNOLOGIES AND SOCIAL MEDIA

> Look for new enabling technologies that create a wide gap between how things have been done and how they can be done.
>
> —*Aaron Levie*

> I fear the day that technology will surpass our human interaction. The world will have a generation of Idiots.
>
> —*Albert Einstein*

This chapter explores how technologies can help with knowledge transfer and innovation, focusing on the core ways they can be used and providing a checklist at the end for our readers. We approach technologies as tools to use as needed and as appropriate in different situations. In themselves, they are not the "be all and end all" to solve problems or create innovation. We simply need to understand what is available and which ones are most appropriate for different situations. However, it is also important to recognize that speed and time of transmission as well as quality and security of the information matter!

There are essentially two types of technologies:

1. Storage technologies such as databases to capture and then access or share valuable knowledge and information.
2. Communication technologies that allow people to share valuable knowledge and information in real time when needed.

However, two other components should be mentioned here:

1. Networks: You need to have a robust (high bandwidth), secure way to transfer the crucial information and knowledge when needed. Therefore, don't

forget to think about what you have, what you need and whether you need to upgrade your networks in order to transfer knowledge quickly and easily.

2. Software: Just like the old saying, "pay no attention to that man behind the curtain" (*The Wizard of Oz*) we often forget about the software that runs everything and assume that things happen "by magic". Therefore, since software changes and new innovative systems improve performance, it is important to remember to stay on top of the software that run your systems.

Here are a couple of theoretical examples to start this discussion:

Technologies can be crucial tools to share valuable information in times of crisis. For example, if you have Marine units that are under attack and the enemy has isolated them, the ability to use the satellite radio or phones for air and land support can mean the difference between life and death for them. And, if they are in remote areas of Afghanistan, you want to be sure that you have invested in robust satellite systems that enable them to communicate clearly and when needed with minimal delays or interruptions in communication.

Similarly, if one unit learns crucial information about the enemy that could save the lives of other units, that information needs to be shared quickly and accurately. In this case, real time communication tools may be needed initially to transmit this new knowledge to an intelligence officer or perhaps to a standard intelligence database. From there, you would probably need good, fast software to recognize the level of urgency of the new knowledge and be able to intelligently push this information through the appropriate channels to get it to other troops who may encounter similar situations. Therefore, they will use both old and new technologies such as telephones (land lines, cellular, satellite), all forms of networks for optimal connectivity, databases to store, search and share information, and emerging Internet software and apps to push the crucial knowledge to the people who need it at the right place and at the right time.

Communication Technologies

A sad example of communication technologies came from the 9/11 attacks: "Cell phones and in-plane credit card phones played a major role during and after the attack, starting with hijacked passengers who called family or notified the authorities about what was happening. Innocent occupants aboard United Airlines Flight 93 were able to assess their situation based on these conversations and planned a revolt that resulted in the aircraft crashing" (National Park Service, 2017). According to the commission staff:

> Because of the quick and determined actions of the passengers and crew, Flight 93 was the only one of the four hijacked aircraft that failed to reach the terrorists' intended target that day. The passengers and crew showed unity, courage, and defiance in the face of adversity.
>
> *(National Park Service, 2017)*

124 Technologies and Social Media

Again, looking at this as a toolkit, what are some of the communication tools available and how can they help with knowledge transfer and innovation?

A review checklist:

1. Synchronous (real time) communication:

    a. Audio: Cell phones, smartphones, radios, satellite phones and similar to provide real time communication and knowledge sharing when needed.

> Even in World War II, we see the huge value of real time communication! This gentleman enlisted in the Army in the infantry division and was given the job of RTO (Radio Telephone Operator, a World War II term). This was an interesting and important position because he communicated with everyone; troops on the ground, headquarters, air support, etc. and acted as a central intelligence hub to keep people safe. He had to learn how to deal with stress and how to communicate information properly; what you say, what you do and who you communicated with were very important. "It was also important to learn to get insights from people at all different levels so that you could act as a translator in communicating effectively with everyone in this job; officers and enlisted; to understand and communicate the pieces of the puzzle and get the big picture to communicate the correct information. Because you had to communicate with a lot of different people who had different perspectives and assumptions, you had to learn these."

    b. Video: Smartphones, laptops, mobile devices, other computers to communicate across the globe anywhere, anytime with both audio and video to capture the context and nuances when needed.
    c. Social media can be synchronous or asynchronous using smartphones, tablets, computers, smartwatches and other devices
    d. Chat: Quick text-based real-time communication using mobile or traditional computer devices.

2. Asynchronous communication: real-time or anytime

    a. Email: To send information or knowledge across the unit or across the globe in a fraction of a second.
    b. Discussion forums: To share and discuss knowledge, projects, problems, etc. including communities of practice. These can include blogs.
    c. Social media: Social media can simulate face-to-face tacit knowledge sharing asynchronously to some extent in the dimensions of social interaction, experience sharing (such as storytelling), observation (often through videos like YouTube), networking and mutual trust.

Technologies and Social Media **125**

d. Knowledge repositories: With good software including artificial intelligence, these database systems can effectively store, manage, search and even disseminate valuable knowledge when needed.

Here is an interesting example from Afghanistan: "Knowledge is also transmitted by email to people who need to learn that new information. In the field, the communication system uses radios and a system called a Blue Force Tracker (BFT) the allows communication via a texting format in many cases. There is a term called COC which stands for command operation center. This is a command center where there are people with needed expertise in different disciplines such as an intelligence officer, an analyst, a medical person, an air person, operations officer and so on so that you have hopefully all the needed experience and knowledge in one room to support you when you are out in the field. You are constantly updating the COC in the field via your BFT and radio. There's something called a TO/E or a "table of organization and equipment" which lists all the weapons and equipment each troop is required to have per job title or billet. All officers are issued weapons, but the true weapon of an officer is his/her radio; not their rifle because knowledge and communication is vital to you being able to operate effectively and control/command their troops in the field or battle.

How Do You Select the Best Technologies?

1. How urgent is the situation?

   a. Critical: Use a form of instant communication such as telephone, radio or live video-chat to get in touch with people immediately.

   b. It is important to share the information or new knowledge, but it is not a life or death situation:

      i. You may need to contact the appropriate person with a chat notification or an email that shows up on their phone/mobile device to let them know that there is some important knowledge or information they need to see.

      ii. If the tacit information cannot be easily shared in a short message, you may need to:

         – arrange for a personal call or video-chat at a specified time
         – provide a link to a specific URL in a database or on a website where they can easily view the message or video.

   c. The information/new knowledge is important to share, but is not mission- or time-critical.

126 Technologies and Social Media

    i.   Create the text or video and store it in a database, on a network or website or similar.

    ii. Send an email to the people who need this information to let them know it is available and should be viewed by a certain time.

2. Is the knowledge or information very dense or complicated?

    a. No—create a report, video, power point presentation, etc. and store it in a database, shared drive, website where people can view it.

    b. Yes—create a video with the supporting multimedia needed to explain the situation as well as possible links for supporting or explanations on the topic or communicate with experts via video-conferencing ideally or via audio (phones).

What Are the Major Technologies Used in the Military?

1. Databases: As discussed in the prior section, the military continuously gathers new knowledge from the after-action reviews (AARs) and ultimately submits the knowledge considered the most important into databases. They also maintain databases of expertise that are available to those seeking expertise in many areas.

2. Networks to share the knowledge successfully. The military maintains high speed networks using fiber optic cable and other technologies to provide fast, secure data transmission within the scope of the Internet. However, they also invest in satellite communications to enable knowledge transfer and communication anywhere, anytime. There are probably many other important technologies which are beyond the scope of this book to discuss.

3. Software to manage the information and knowledge, applications to categorize it and provide sophisticated searchable content with security built in. There are specialized applications like sensors and detections software, sophisticated software to run equipment, but for knowledge storage and transfer, companies work with the military to provide advanced solutions. For example, "An important KM tool is the Global Information Grid— the globally interconnected, end-to-end set of information capabilities, associated processes for collecting, processing, storing, disseminating, and managing information on demand to warfighters, policy makers, and support personnel. The Global Information Grid includes owned and leased communications and computing systems and services, software (including applications), data, security services, other associated services, and National Security Systems" (Army Pubs, 2013).

4. Social media: The military has recognized the value of social media. As far back as 2002, the military recognized the value of using the first social media tools for effective knowledge transfer. "One of the best examples of the growing acceptance of a knowledge-based culture is the creation of a U.S. Army blog site called CompanyCommander.com. The initial concept was developed in 2002 by two

U.S. Army officers who realized the value of sharing experiences and lessons learned from time spent in Iraq. The rapid acceptance and use of the site lead U.S. Army leadership to officially endorse, resource, and expand the concept into CompanyCommand.army.mil" (U.S. Strategic Command Office, 2009).

As discussed in Chapter 6, they also integrate that new knowledge into their continual live and online training exercises.

What About Technologies in Business?

The goal is to provide easy, convenient tools that help people share valuable knowledge when they need it. Therefore, the basic ones discussed are still valuable here.

However, on a more general note, businesses can consider some other technologies to stay on a competitive playing field (Northeast Dealers, 2015; Gartner, 2017):

1. Cloud technologies: While the military has big budgets for hardware, software and IT expertise, many businesses benefit by focusing their resources on their core competencies and outsourcing hardware and software to experts by using cloud services and applications.

Benefits of cloud systems:

- No need to invest funds in hardware, software or IT personnel.
- Cyber security is taken care of by the cloud provider.
- Cloud apps such as logistics, customer relationship management, HR/expertise, etc. are updated regularly and also provide mobility to personnel.
- Ability to scale the systems such as adding new apps when needed, adding capacity when needed.

Communication and collaboration systems use emerging software to enhance knowledge sharing. For example, there are cloud-based software solutions on the market that create a unified communication-collaboration portal. These are some of the things an information system like this can do:

a. Internal communications with chat apps, internal social media channels, and mobile accessibility to all knowledge throughout the organization.
b. Cloud directory with smart software to find needed expertise throughout the organization.
c. Collaboration pages that allow people to work together on projects from across the globe.
d. Knowledge repositories with intelligent tagging to easily search and find needed information and knowledge.

128 Technologies and Social Media

Another example of a newer cloud-based real-time software would be something like slack.com, which is a cloud-based messaging system that allows you to create different "channels" for different projects. You can have public or private chat channels, can integrate your social media feeds into it, and can communicate and collaborate in real time or asynchronously.

2. Big data, databases, artificial intelligence and analytics: Innovation is driven by new knowledge creation. By using the emerging capabilities of sophisticated software algorithms, you can leverage the immense power of computers and artificial intelligence (AI) to give your efforts a boost. For example, IBM's "Watson" is an AI system that is like having thousands of colleagues working on a new knowledge initiative simultaneously. Here is an interesting example in healthcare where using Watson is like having MANY doctors communicating and collaborating in research and diagnosis (Forrest, 2015):

> The medical field is the sector that is likely being impacted the most by Watson. For starters, Watson has taken residence at three of the top cancers hospitals in the U.S.—Memorial Sloan Kettering Cancer Center, University of Texas MD Anderson Cancer Center, and the Mayo Clinic—where it helps with cancer research and patient care. In terms of cancer research, Watson is speeding up DNA analysis in cancer patients to help make their treatment more effective.
>
> For physicians, Watson is helping with diagnoses. A dermatology app called schEMA allows doctors to input patient data and, using natural-language processing (NLP), helps identify potential symptoms and treatments. Additionally, Watson uses vision recognition to help doctors read scans such as X-rays and MRIs to better narrow the focus on a potential ailment.

3. Mobile, Internet of Things (IoT) and Apps: Mobile devices are becoming the norm with consumers and businesses using them for virtually every transaction and most communication. People need to communicate and collaborate anywhere, anytime. Therefore, making sure that your people have mobile tools and technologies makes it easier to share knowledge and create innovation. Similarly, mobile apps are creating huge improvements in innovation via productivity tools, knowledge sharing systems and new emerging ways of connecting people-to-people or people-to-businesses. In addition, the Internet of Things (IoT)(see Figure 8.1) represents a new way for the world to become interconnected via sensors connected to the Internet and to artificial intelligence to manage these interconnected systems.

According to Forrester research, by the end of 2017, U.S mobile users will spend $90 billion via mobile payments. That is a 48% increase over the $12.8 billion spent in 2012. Gartner forecasted that in 2017 U.S consumers' mobile engagement behavior will push up mobile commerce revenue to 50 percent of U.S. digital commerce revenue.

B2B marketers are now increasingly leveraging the mobile commerce to push up sales. B2B generates 19.4% of digital commerce revenue from mobile channels compared to B2C's 22.6%. Though less, B2B is poised to outrun B2C in mobile commerce in short time because 50% B2B buyers are tech-savvy, young mobile users who are decision makers, influencers or stakeholders.

The reports confirmed that mobile users spent more time on apps compared to mobile web. The 86:14 (app:mobile web usage) ratio shows that apps dominate the mobile shopping time. Since users spend more time on the apps, the apps drive more converting traffic to mobile commerce sites. A survey by Criteo found out that retail mobile apps convert 3.7 times more than mobile web (Perception, 2016).

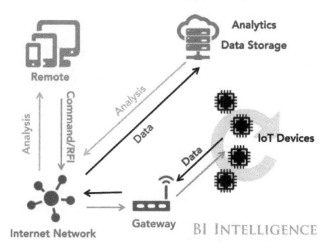

FIGURE 8.1 The Internet of Things

Source: Business Insider, 2016: www.businessinsider.com/iot-ecosystem-internet-of-things-forecasts-and-business-opportunities-2016-2

According to Business Insider (2016), the IoT will become a source for competitive advantage for both business and government:

- In total, we project there will be 34 billion devices connected to the internet by 2020, up from 10 billion in 2015. IoT devices will account for 24 billion, while traditional computing devices (e.g. smartphones, tablets, smartwatches, etc.) will comprise 10 billion.
- Nearly $6 trillion will be spent on IoT solutions over the next five years.
- Businesses will be the top adopter of IoT solutions. They see three ways the IoT can improve their bottom line by 1) lowering operating costs; 2) increasing productivity; and 3) expanding to new markets or developing new product offerings.
- Governments are focused on increasing productivity, decreasing costs, and improving their citizens' quality of life. We believe they will be the second-largest adopters of IoT ecosystems.

4. Security: Cyber security is becoming a crucial element in knowledge transfer. You have to trust that the valuable information and knowledge that you are sharing will be secure. You do *not* want valuable intelligence to fall into enemy hands; whether you are in the military or in business. Therefore, the moral of the story is to be vigilant and take cyber security seriously!

5. Social media: Is it really that important? Yes. With the explosion of social media in all aspects of business and daily lives, most organizations now recognize its value. "65% of respondents of global business executives say their organizations use social business tools to understand market shifts; 45% to improve visibility into operations; and 45% to identify internal talent" (Kiron et al., 2013). It is probably safe to say that most people feel comfortable using social media. Therefore, using it as either a synchronous or asynchronous way to share knowledge represents an important part of the technology mix. And, don't forget that more and more people are using social media on their mobile devices! However, we also caution against the "build it and they will come" approach (*Field of Dreams*, 1989). Rather, as discussed in the chapter on culture, the most important thing a business should focus on is to build relationships and trust where people feel comfortable sharing their valuable knowledge. Then, the social media simply serves as an easy, familiar channel to share that knowledge.

- 97 percent of online adults aged 16–64 say they have visited or used a social network within the last month.
- 8 in 10 internet users globally visit/use social networks on their mobile devices.
- People are most likely to use social media in order to keep up with friends (43 %) or news (41 %), or to fill time (39 %).
- Around 1 in every 3 minutes spent online is devoted to social networking and messaging, with digital consumers engaging for a daily average of 1 hour and 58 minutes.

(Mansfield, 2016)

Social Media Revisited

It is no surprise to anyone that social media has transformed the way we live and do business. According to Social Media Today:

- 22% of the world's population use Facebook, and 76% of those users logged in every day in 2016
- On any given day, Snapchat reaches 41% of 18–34 year olds in the U.S.
- 81% of Millennials check Twitter at least once a day
- 80% of time spent on social media happens on a mobile device.

(Ahmad, 2017)

In an interesting article (Huang, 2011) about the Arab Spring uprising, several major social media platforms, including Facebook and Twitter, were credited with making this social movement a reality. For example, "During the protests in Egypt and Tunisia, the vast majority of 200-plus people surveyed over three weeks in March said they were getting their information from social media sites (88 per cent in Egypt and 94 per cent in Tunisia)" (Huang, 2011).

Another interesting article in the Guardian (Beaumont, 2011), describes some "defining moments" with social media including:

> He is an angry Egyptian doctor in an aid station stooping to capture the image of a man with a head injury from missiles thrown by Mubarak's supporters. Or it is a Libyan in Benghazi running with his phone switched to a jerky video mode, surprised when the youth in front of him is shot through the head.

As someone "on the ground" in the midst of the uprising, he gives the following report.

"Social media was absolutely crucial," says Koubaa. "Three months before Mohammed Bouazizi burned himself in Sidi Bouzid we had a similar case in Monastir. But no one knew about it because it was not filmed. What made a difference this time is that the images of Bouazizi were put on Facebook and everybody saw it."

"In Egypt, details of demonstrations were circulated by both Facebook and Twitter and the activists' 12-page guide to confronting the regime was distributed by email."

"But above all it has been about the ability to communicate. Egyptian-born blogger Mona Eltahawy says that social media has given the most marginalised groups in the region a voice. To say 'Enough' and 'This is how I feel.'"

132 Technologies and Social Media

What About the Impact Social Media Has Had on Business?

According to Roberts (2017), an interesting study by CISCO revealed:

> "A Cisco study predicted that mobile video traffic will account for 75 per cent of total mobile data traffic by 2020. Video is arguably the future of social media and, according to the Social Media Marketing Industry Report 2016, 73 per cent of marketers plan on increasing their use of video in 2017, and 50 per cent plan on using live video in their marketing.
>
> But how many will incorporate Snapchat into their video strategy? Data released last April revealed that users of the app were watching 10 billion videos per day. That figure had grown from 8 billion in just two months, and will likely continue growing as we move into 2017. Any brands continuing to omit Snapchat from their marketing strategy should make 2017 the year they get involved."

He also reports that with Microsoft's recent acquisition of LinkedIn, their market value will reach $1 trillion and they will enhance internal business operations via a LinkedIn "Business News Desk" that will facilitate internal communications and knowledge transfer.

Another interesting business opportunity is "chatbots". For example, Facebook has actively incorporated them into its Facebook messenger. He states, in terms of chatbots, "This growth is reflected in the increasing popularity of messaging apps, which are growing faster than social networks and fueling the rise of chatbots in the process." The value to business is the ability to reach customers in a more personal way either using live chat within a website or social media or these more automated artificial intelligent chatbots.

> "Chat bots are computer programs that mimic conversation with people using artificial intelligence" (Wong, 2016).

Instagram also showed significant growth, adding business pages and other features. "All that progress tempted 100 million new users into downloading the app to join the 500 million already on board" (Roberts, 2017).

These are recent trends. However, the moral of the story for business is the concept of "digital Darwinism" (Solis, 2016). The meaning is essentially "innovate or die". He describes this as

> disruptive technology's effect on business and society. It's a modern-day take of creative destruction through the lens of disruptive technology. The effect

of digital Darwinism on Corporate America is real, and it's enlivened though evolutionary changes in people (customers, employees, and business partners)—how they think, learn, and make decisions; what they expect, prefer, and value; how they influence and are influenced.

Lessons Learned—Military or Business:

Social media is huge and growing. The same is true today for cloud-based systems and mobile systems. However, this may change tomorrow. The point is that if your business does not constantly monitor and keep up with these changing technologies, your competitors will and you will possibly go into a "death spiral".

For example, an official at the Pentagon recently warned that

> Potential adversaries are challenging the U.S. lead in conventional military capability in ways not seen since the Cold War. U.S. commanders are already worried about sophisticated air defenses and anti-ship missiles. But officials said other countries are devoting efforts to creating precision-guided rockets and artillery that could possibly target biometric signatures, massive cyber warfare and systems that link soldiers with various robotic weaponry.
>
> *(Phys.org, 2015)*

Once again, this recognition of keeping up with changing technologies also involves a cultural shift where top military leaders also recognize the urgent need to learn and adapt continually. "The reform initiative called for scaling back bureaucratic rules, attracting technically-savvy workers to oversee programs and designing weapons so that technological advances can be quickly added" (Phys.org, 2015). Never-ending innovation is key! Here is a great example from Afghanistan:

In Afghanistan, an Air Force guy set up a system using Google Earth where he created overlays with a common naming scheme. For example, if someone went on patrol and talked to someone at intersection 1, he could take a picture of the person and summarize the conversation and keep going. If he then saw an IED in an orchard, he could record the details of this, etc. When he got back, he could go onto Google Earth and create an overlay, perhaps called "Patrol 1" which would describe the events such as putting an icon of an IED at the orchard with a description, a picture of the guy and the interview at intersection 1, etc. This would create a graphical picture of what was happening and you could see pictures of the IEDs to create a pattern analysis. This can be amazingly powerful; you can layer shape files and create a holistic view from different perspectives to show what was happening and could then point, click and share this with other commanders who were geographically dispersed.

134 Technologies and Social Media

Moral of the Story?

In business, as in the military, you need to be able to communicate when needed and with the right people. You also need to be able to share important information and knowledge; store it, and make it easily accessible to others who can use it. Therefore, use database systems that are user-friendly, available to people in many formats; e.g. on-site as well as mobile, and well managed. Information overload is just as bad as not having the information or knowledge that you need. Therefore, having IT and IS people dedicated to understanding the organization's needs and keeping up with the technologies to provide the best communication and access to valuable information and knowledge is crucial. Be proactive about finding the right communication technologies to fit the situation; see prior checklist.

And now for a little theory:

As discussed earlier in the chapter, technologies change rapidly and with digital technologies, artificial intelligence and the Internet, the speed of innovation and change becomes overwhelming. Therefore, the purpose of this chapter is not to share specific technologies with you, but rather to encourage an attitude of continual learning, adaptation and leveraging of current and emerging technologies to keep you on your "A-game".

One of the classic theories along these lines comes from a book by Everett M. Rogers (2003), *Diffusion of Innovations*. In this foundational work, he explored the many dimensions associated with the adoption and diffusion of innovations. He suggests that

> there are four main elements influencing the adoption and diffusion of innovations including: (1) the innovation, (2) communication channels, (3) time, and (4) the social systems. To break this down into greater detail, he suggests that there are five main attributes of innovations that can predict an innovation's rate of adoption, (a) The relative advantage of an innovation (the degree to which the innovation is perceived as better than the idea it supercedes) is positively related to its rate of adoption and continued and effective use. (b) The perceived compatibility (the degree to which an innovation is perceived as consistent with the existing values, past experiences, and needs of potential adopters) of an innovation is positively related to its rate of adoption and continued and effective use. (c) The perceived complexity (the degree to which an innovation is perceived as relatively difficult to understand and to use) of an innovation is negatively related to its rate of adoption, (d) The perceived triability (the degree to which an innovation may be experimented with on a limited basis) is positively related to its rate of adoption, (e) The perceived observability (the degree to which the results of an innovation are visible to others) is positively related to its rate of adoption.
>
> *(Jones, 2001)*

There have been many subsequent studies to refine and elaborate on these classic models. Many researchers have validated the importance of relative advantage in the adoption process. Relative advantage is usually defined as the perception of a new innovation as superior to current offerings and has been validated as the best predictor of innovation adoption. Interestingly, some researchers have expanded the view of relative advantage to include specific attributes that are most important to the target market users. This includes the resulting impacts from the new innovation on work performance, but is also mitigated by factors of trust; basically in the credibility of the source of the innovation (Choudhury and Karahanna, 2008). These researchers also suggest that social cognitive theory (SCT) should also be considered when exploring whether people will adopt new innovations. SCT suggests that individuals' experiences, beliefs, values and motives greatly influence their decisions. Therefore, as discussed in Chapter 4, a cohesive culture with strong shared norms and values will also contribute to the successful adoption and diffusion of innovations if the culture emphasizes continual learning, a quest for new knowledge and the benefits of relative advantage and change.

Another widely accepted theory is called the Technology Acceptance Model (TAM). In this model, researchers suggest that the adoption of an innovation is influenced by its perceived ease of use and perceived usefulness (Davis, 1993). Perceived usefulness is similar to relative advantage; how will this new technology better impact the user's performance? Perceived ease of use involves the perception of how much time and work it will take to learn and use this new technology. The TAM has been empirically tested over the years by many researchers and found to exert a profound and significant impact on technology/innovation adoption and use (Kansal, 2016).

What is the Internet of Things (IoT)? "This is the concept of basically connecting any device with an on and off switch to the Internet (and/or to each other). This includes everything from cellphones, coffee makers, washing machines, headphones, lamps, wearable devices and almost anything else you can think of. This also applies to components of machines, for example a jet engine of an airplane or the drill of an oil rig. As I mentioned, if it has an on and off switch then chances are it can be a part of the IoT. The analyst firm Gartner says that by 2020 there will be over 26 billion connected devices. . . . That's a lot of connections (some even estimate this number to be much higher, over 100 billion). The IoT is a giant network of connected 'things' (which also includes people). The relationship will be between people-people, people-things, and things-things" (Morgan, 2014).

In an interesting article by Lyytinen et al. (2016), an entirely new way of thinking about information technologies is suggested. Rather than focusing on technologies

136 Technologies and Social Media

and their impact on a product, process or system, they argue that the world is evolving into a global network. For example, with the IoT (Internet of Things – see box above for definition), the world is becoming an interconnected constellation of heterogeneous networks with almost limitless knowledge available to people who navigate them. They suggest that innovation occurs through these webs of social and technological interactions. While these vast external networks will have social, political and power complexities, the potential for knowledge creation and knowledge sharing for ultimate innovation is immense. Digital convergence in the form of knowledge shared by people or machine to machine data exchange, mediated by artificial intelligence to harness the trends, patterns and cumulative information across the globe, which has huge potential for continual innovation. An example could be within the automotive industry. With sensors monitoring many aspects of the driving experience and sending the resulting data back to databases via the IoT, the potential for global design increases tremendously. If engineers have access to these huge data warehouses equipped with artificial intelligence to analyze the vast data from potentially millions of cars, they could innovate with engine design, fuel efficiencies, safety designs and more. Another example discussed by Lyytinen et al. (2016) is Google.

> Google's strategic goal is to use digital technologies as a shared platform to allow continuous innovation in a large number of user communities and to integrate knowledge communities into an innovation ecology. Its main strategy is to leverage open standards and open-access principles in a quest to offer services that allow users to search digital content in any form. They actively seek to utilize their digital platform for integrating and innovating with diverse communities. Their digital infrastructure allows Google to quickly integrate newly acquired services into their core offering. In addition, Google uses a bottom-up approach to innovation in which most employees are entitled to use up to 20% of their time to explore ideas based on the digital platform.
>
> *(pp. 63–64).*

In the next chapter, we wrap this all up and attempt to put all of these moving pieces on the puzzle into a model that makes sense to help your business improve your crucial knowledge transfer and ability to innovate continually for sustainable competitive advantage!

Veteran Quotes: Veterans' Perspectives on Technologies and Social Media

Global War on Terror (GWOT); Iraq

- In these meetings with the local leaders he would be transcribing the meeting but he would also be on the radio and in communication with the people on the outside; troops, air support etc. so that he could communicate what was happening and know if they needed to leave at any time.

GWOT; Afghanistan

- There are knowledge managers at the Battalion level who manage the SharePoint databases, but this often does not work well because the databases are clunky and the IT people do not often have the training to recognize the knowledge in order to categorize it correctly. Therefore, it can be very difficult to search and access the knowledge that is needed.

References

Ahmad, I. (2017). "30+ Marketing Stats for 2017 [Infographic]", available at www. socialmediatoday.com/social-business/30-social-media-marketing-stats-2017-infographic (accessed April, 2017).

Army Pubs. (2013). "Mission Command Center of Excellence: Doctrine Update", available at http://armypubs.army.mil/doctrine/DR_pubs/DR_a/pdf/fm6_01x1.pdf 2013, (accessed on July 8, 2016).

Beaumont, P. (2011). "The Truth about Twitter, Facebook and the Uprisings in the Arab World", *The Guardian*, February 25, available at www.theguardian.com/world/2011/feb/25/twitter-facebook-uprisings-arab-libya (accessed February 17, 2017).

Business Insider. (2016). "Here Are IoT Trends That Will Change the Way Businesses, Governments, and Consumers Interact with the World", available at www. businessinsider.com/top-internet-of-things-trends-2016-1 (accessed April 2, 2017).

Choudhury, V. and Karahanna, E. (2008). "The relative advantage of electronic channels: A multidimensional view." *MIS Quarterly*, Vol. 32 No. 1: 179–200.

Davis, F. D. (1993). "User acceptance of information technology: System characteristics, user perceptions and behavioral impacts." *International Journal of Man-Machine Studies*, Vol. 38 No. 3: 475–487.

Field of Dreams (film). (1989). Universal Pictures.

Forrest, C. (2015). "IBM Watson: What Are Companies Using It for?", available at www.zdnet.com/article/ibm-watson-what-are-companies-using-it-for/ (accessed September 23, 2016).

Gartner, Inc. (2017). "Top 10 Strategic Technology Trends for 2017", available at www. gartner.com/technology/research/top-10-technology-trends/ (accessed March 23, 2017).

Huang, C. (2011). "Facebook and Twitter Key to Arab Spring Uprisings: Report", *The National*, June 6, available at www.thenational.ae/news/uae-news/facebook-and-twitter-key-to-arab-spring-uprisings-report (accessed February 17, 2017).

Jones, N. B. (2001). "The Diffusion of a Collaborative CSCW Technology to Facilitate Knowledge Sharing and Performance Improvement", Dissertation, University of Missouri: UMI, ProQuest Information and Learning.

Kansal, P. (2016). "Perceived risk and technology acceptance model in self-service banking: A study on the nature of mediation." *South Asian Journal of Management*, Vol. 23 No. 2: 51–71.

Kiron, D., Palmer, D., Nguyen, A. P. and Berkman, R. (2013). "Social Business Study: Shifting out of First Gear", Deloitte University Press, July 16, available at https://dupress.deloitte.com/dup-us-en/topics/emerging-technologies/social-business-study.html (accessed June, 2016).

Lyytinen, K., Yoo, Y. and Boland, R. J. Jr. (2016). "Digital product innovation within four classes of innovation networks." *Information Systems Journal*, Vol. 26: 47–75.

138 Technologies and Social Media

Morgan, J. (2014). "A Simple Explanation of 'The Internet of Things'", available at www.forbes.com/sites/jacobmorgan/2014/05/13/simple-explanation-internet-things-that-anyone-can-understand/#8b9f7e11d091 (accessed on April 19, 2017).

National Park Service. (2017). "The Flight 93 Story", available at www.nps.gov/flni/learn/historyculture/index.htm (accessed January, 2018).

Northeast Dealers. (2015). "Essential Technologies Every Business Needs in 2015", available at http://nedealers.com/essential-technologies-every-business-needs-in-2015/ (accessed December 3, 2015).

Perception (2016). "Mobile Commerce Trends 2017: Opportunities and Challenges with Statistics", available at http://blogs.perceptionsystem.com/mobile-commerce-trends-2017/ (accessed March 3, 2016).

Phys.org (2015). "US Military Worries About Losing Hi-tech Edge", available at http://phys.org/news/2015-04-military-hi-tech-edge.html (accessed April 20, 2016).

Roberts, P. (2017). "8 Social Media Statistics for 2017", available at http://oursocialtimes.com/7-social-media-statistics-for-2017/ (accessed February 18, 2017).

Rogers, E. M. (2003). *Diffusion of Innovations* (5th edition). New York: The Free Press.

Solis, B. (2016). "MarketWatch: This Is How the Smartest Companies Are Leading the Tech (R)evolution", available at www.briansolis.com/tag/digital-darwinism/ (accessed February 18, 2017).

U.S. Strategic Command Office. (2009). "Knowledge Transfer Book", available at http://usacac.army.mil/cac2/AOKM/Knowledge%20Transfer%20Book.pdf (accessed February 21, 2016).

The Wizard of Oz (film). (1939). Metro-Goldwyn-Mayer (MGM), USA.

Wong, J. (2016). "What Is a Chat Bot, and Should I Be Using One?", available at www.theguardian.com/technology/2016/apr/06/what-is-chat-bot-kik-bot-shop-messaging-platform (accessed May, 2017).

9

PUTTING IT ALL TOGETHER

What have we learned from all of this and how can it help our businesses be more competitive as well as aid individuals in both the performance of their jobs and professional growth?

1. Leadership and culture. It all starts here. The leaders of an organization often have an enormous amount of power. With that power comes a huge responsibility to establish a culture that nurtures respect, collaboration, and values all employees. They also must actively promote shared goals and a desire to make a difference and contribute to the mission in a meaningful way. Dr. Mylea Charvat (2017), founder and CEO of Savonix observed "One of the biggest lessons I have learned is that it is hard for many people to tell truth to power." She further observes that most "company cultures have a 'kill the messenger' culture that discourages people from identifying risks and problems effectively".

2. Other leadership and cultural issues to focus on the following:

    a. The culture needs to be flexible and adaptive where the leaders develop a structure and incentives that support innovation, change, collaboration, knowledge sharing and risk-taking.

    b. Leaders need to communicate a clear and compelling mission and vision to colleagues while helping them adapt to changes. This occurs via innovation and creativity and an environment that embraces a philosophy of continual learning, knowledge sharing and helping each other.

    c. Leaders can model this by communicating frequently with everyone in the organization, sharing important information and knowledge and creating a "transparent" organization where most information and knowledge is open and accessible and secrecy is actively discouraged.

140 Putting It All Together

d. Leaders also need to develop trust, openness and communication in addition to helping to develop strong bonds of trust and strong relationships to create cohesive teams and social networks. This helps to build strong teams where people enjoy and appreciate each other and "have each other's backs". If we look at the military, because they live and work together so intensively, their units become a "band of brothers". This is something worth working towards in business. Consider your personal "credibility" and reputation as you lead your organization and influence others. The small table shows the impacts of doing what you say you will do; or conversely not doing what you say you will not do. In transfer of knowledge, credibility is important (recall the earlier discussion on knowledge corruption).

Commitment	To take action	To not take action
TAKE ACTION	Credible behavior	Not credible behavior
NOT ACT	Not credible behavior	Credible behavior

Note that we are not arguing for the evaluation of the action or non-action in term of its effectiveness, rightness or any other criteria other than: do you do what you said you would do (or did not do what you said you would not do). So if you ask a colleague to support you, and she does, that is a credible behavior and action—building trust and credibility with you. If you ask someone not to do something and they do, they have engaged in untrustworthy behavior and action. Is your behavior, over the long term, credible? As leaders you *must* walk the walk in your organization.

e. Develop a culture where people are hungry for knowledge; they see the value in always seeking to learn more, to find new, better ways of doing things, to learn from each other as well as outside the organization so that everyone's knowledge base is always increasing and innovation becomes the norm. This creates a win-win for everyone since each employee increases their expertise and knowledge making them more valuable and the organization creates collaborative people with great expertise who can work together to create continual innovation for better products, services and processes, creating sustainable competitive advantage!

3. Training: We believe this is perhaps the greatest strength of the military and the greatest on-going weakness of businesses.

a. Start with a commitment to education and training and invest in a "boot camp"-type experience for every associate. This will create a shared culture, develop relationships as well as a deep understanding of the mission and vision of the organization. It will also create cohesive bonds that will continue to grow throughout the organization; necessary for effective collaboration to create innovation. Many of the best training programs (in terms of lasting impact, socialization and team building) are of the "boot camp" variety. It is crucial, we believe, in consideration of training to leverage the individual's experiences to help everyone in the organization get better.

b. Similarly, invest in continual training/education for associates analogous to the continual training done by the military after "boot camp". This provides a sustainable vehicle for people to learn and then share important new knowledge about the environment, customers, competitors, new emerging trends, or technologies. It also provides associates with continual growth and development that will keep them interested, engaged and motivated to work towards the shared mission of innovation for sustainable competitive advantage. A missed opportunity is the training/education of older workers. The mythology is that they cannot adapt or learn new things. This is just that, a prevalent myth.

c. Training not only provides education in terms of skills and expertise, but perhaps more importantly, it provides socialization, which is necessary to create strong bonds of trust and collaboration.

d. Training also helps to create "shared meaning" where people learn about each other; their personalities, nuances, meaning so that they can communicate clearly regardless of prior experiences, social class or education. They also gain expertise in different areas which makes them more valuable. As mentioned in the prior section, with the combination of effective communication and continual learning and expertise, business can potentially create a sustainable competitive advantage with the resulting continual innovation from these people.

The intense acculturation achieved in Marine boot camp is a good example of this. In order to have true shared meaning in crisis situations, people need to develop strong relationships and trust, have many commonalities and understand each other's nuances and communication patterns. This socialization also encourages a shift in identity where members see themselves as part of a team, which leads to cohesiveness and tacit knowledge sharing. Colleagues feel a sense of responsibility for each other . . . they "have each other's backs" and want to help the team and the organization achieve their mission and goals. Therefore, businesses should invest in training "boot camps" for all associates to gain the socialization and education necessary for a cohesive team who can share knowledge, understand each other and attain organization goals and mission.

e. Businesses should learn to use the after-action reviews (AARs) that have been so helpful and successful in the military. As one Army intelligence

142 Putting It All Together

officer mentioned, the AARs become ingrained into the routines. After each patrol, you do an AAR to see what you learned, what worked, and what did not and incorporate the most important lesson or two into your next patrol, which could be 10 minutes later. Continual training for all employees should become institutionalized throughout the organization.

4. Remove barriers and reduce knowledge corruption:

   a. Rewards and incentives: Since leaders have the authority to create rewards and incentives within the organization, they can create rewards for collaboration and sharing valuable knowledge. For example, performance evaluation systems can evaluate both team and individual performance with a laser-focus on achievement of the mission and vision in all performance metrics. If a team works effectively together to create new innovations in products or processes, everyone will benefit; the organization as well as the team members.

   b. Constantly evaluate your knowledge processes and be sensitive to situations where knowledge hoarding can occur in your organization. Reward and recognize sharing of knowledge throughout the organization on a continual basis.

   c. Returning to the value of great leaders: None of this will work unless you have leaders who are trustworthy and who value the attainment of the organizational mission and goals over personal power or political agendas. Leaders must also be willing to share their knowledge and promote a culture of sharing rather than hoarding. Many of our Veterans were adamant that good leaders are humble; they promote a culture of trust and respect and they truly value their people. If leaders possess a "we know everything" attitude with a good dose of arrogance, they will certainly alienate their people and destroy any attempt at knowledge sharing and innovation. Great leaders "walk the walk" rather than "talk the talk".

5. Develop a solid structure to capture, store and share knowledge:

   a. As mentioned, business can learn from the military by developing the equivalent of routine AARs (after-action reviews). While businesses are famous for meetings, they can change the focus to task-oriented, project-oriented, mission-driven pre-planning sessions and after-action reviews. This allows the organization to set specific, quantifiable goals and action plans and then learn what happened to capture the knowledge of the different people involved.

   b. Provide people with the tools and technologies to communicate effectively and share knowledge in the moment as well as afterwards. In military crisis situations, this included radios, a command center to monitor

Putting it all Together **143**

and respond to intelligence from different sources and the ability to respond immediately with needed support, knowledge and resources. In business, this could involve the use of social media as well as other collaborative platforms to encourage collaboration and knowledge sharing with software to capture and share the critical new knowledge created. This also involves a good technology structure with effective database systems, networks, mobile apps and business intelligence.

c. Develop a structure to send information and knowledge gained up the channels to SMEs (subject matter experts) who can evaluate and filter the abundance of knowledge that is created and shared. See Figure 1.1 in Chapter 1 for a model.

d. As mentioned, create a robust database system to collect, categorize and share this knowledge with sophisticated search software. This should include sections for lessons learned, stories, videos, and capturing social media content.

We are convinced that the future of organizational success is tied deeply to knowledge management and that successful knowledge management reinforces innovation and innovation serves as a catalyst for new knowledge. Consider all of the jobs and skills that have been eliminated or significantly transformed in the last twenty years as a consequence of new knowledge and innovation. According to Eric Hoffer: "In times of drastic change it is the learners who inherit the future. The learned usually find themselves equipped to live in a world that no longer exists" (Hoffer, 2006). As a consequence, organizations, as well as employees must engage in a continual process of learning.

If you can incorporate these lessons into your culture and structure of the organization, you can effectively create new knowledge within your ranks, develop a culture of innovation and knowledge appreciation. You can then develop effective ways to make this knowledge available to the people throughout the organization for collaboration and continual innovation for success!

References

Charvat, M. (2017). "Creating a Values-Based Culture vs. 'Bro Culture' in Silicon Valley", August 16, available at www.linkedin.com/pulse/creating-values-based-culture-vs-bro-silicon-valley-charvat-ph-d-?trk=v-%20feed&lipi=urn%3Ali%3Apage%3Ad_flagship3_detail_base%3BrzrjVj%2Femo4kW8EwJbdBZw%3D%3D (accessed September, 2017).

Hoffer, E. (2006). *Reflections on the Human Condition*. Titusville, NJ: Hopewell Publications.

10

A "ROSETTA STONE" FOR MILITARY SKILLS TRANSLATION TO BUSINESS

The Veterans who shared their valuable insights with us asked if we could similarly share our business insights with them in a specific way. Because the worlds of the military and business are very different, they asked if we would attempt to create a translation vehicle; a "Rosetta stone" to translate the amazing skills and competencies they developed and learned in the military into the business equivalents. This is our attempt.

Skills/competencies in greatest demand by businesses:

1. Communication
2. Leadership
3. Critical thinking
4. Complex problem-solving
5. Judgment and decision-making
6. Teamwork
7. Motivation and strong work ethic
8. Positive attitude
9. Specific knowledge and ability to learn
10. Initiative, self-motivation, drive
11. Planning, organizing, prioritizing
12. Flexibility, being adaptable
13. Time management
14. Global perspective
15. Integrity, honesty
16. Professionalism
17. Creativity, innovativeness

Translation to Business Skills/Competencies

Here is an attempt at a business translation. Note that we are using the sentences straight from our interviews with the Veterans. Therefore, while this will not look as polished or business professional as you might expect, the goal is to show the valuable knowledge and skills that these Veterans gained in these mission-critical competencies. Thus, a business leader can see how Veterans can add great value to their organization. We assume that the combat Veterans we interviewed would have similar skills, competencies and knowledge as most Veterans in their situations.

1. Communication:

   a. Learned to communicate with different people, different cultures; effective communication mattered in life and death situations.
   b. Learned how to streamline the communications so that you know what to communicate; e.g. the most important information.
   c. Learned how to analyze all variables, prioritize most important, filter out the "noise" and communicate quickly and effectively the most crucial information in crisis situations.

2. Leadership:

   a. Learned to make good decisions under pressure and communicate well.
   b. Being humble, not asking your team to do anything you would not do, empathy, sincere concern for your team, learn everything, start strong, learn as much as possible, and communicating well.

3. Critical thinking, analysis, decision-making, complex problem-solving:

   a. Intense training to assess complex situations, prioritize information most relevant to situation and make decisions, often under crisis conditions.
   b. In the intensive training as well as in the field, learned to analyze complex situations quickly in real time, remain calm under intense pressure and be able to assess different situations to find optimal solutions and decisions.
   c. Trained to be self-sufficient and was empowered to make mission-critical decisions at any time.
   d. Most Veterans in leadership positions learned complex planning, operational management and strategy equivalent to top level managers and executives in business.

4. Teamwork:

   a. Trained and worked with many different types of people.
   b. Learned to adapt and work effectively in multi-disciplinary teams, communicate in teams, develop organizational skills, team management, planning, prioritizing and accomplishing the mission as a team to get everyone home safe and alive.

146 Military Skills Translation to Business

5. Other skills and competencies:

   a. Confidence
   b. Assertiveness
   c. Ability to be bold
   d. Language skills
   e. Strategy
   f. Teamwork
   g. Writing reports, communicating
   h. Professionalism, respect, integrity, honor
   i. Discipline, self-motivation, adaptability, flexibility

Other skills mentioned by Veterans:

- Confidence, assertiveness, ability to be bold; Veterans do not get scared; they put it all on the line, they are not afraid anymore, and they are not afraid to try.
- Computer skills, language skills, strategy, teamwork, writing reports, communicating; appropriate and effective.
- Professionalism, respect, discipline.
- How to think; the ability to work as a team and also as an individual; how to adapt to a situation (always had to adapt to different leaders).
- Scenarios: you have to be able to look at different scenarios and deal with things under pressure, no matter what happens, adapt, deal with the pressure, and keep moving forward.
- Simulate high stress situations in a controlled environment many times. If you do this with some people who you will be working with in the field, you learn how to communicate with them and also learn how to streamline the communications so that you know what to communicate; e.g. the most important information. You also learn to become "hardened"; this also comes with experience—the better you are able to cope with a stressful situation and still communicate effectively and accurately (quality of the communication), the better the end result. Time and clarity is of the essence and often emotions take control and you may communicate "noise" instead of crucial information. However, in crisis situations, you need to share the critical information, so you need to learn to reduce the noise (the unnecessary information) and distill the core, important information: (sometimes called "muscle memory").
- Remaining calm and in control even under a lot of stress. You recognize that you have to maintain control of your emotions to ensure that there will be success in the mission; this can save lives. You have to learn to be calm under pressure; clear thinking; learn to think critically and analytically to make sound decisions.

- As a leader, you have to learn to make these decisions under pressure. Part of this is the training; learn to control emotions so that you don't make bad decisions. You also need to learn to communicate these decisions to others.
- Leadership: start strong; gain as much knowledge as possible; embrace the initial period of learning; "drinking through a fire hose". It will give you the insights needed.
- Be a physical leader; do their jobs to understand what they do; their perspectives; how to communicate with them; learn the different roles.
- Other comments from Veterans about this:

  - Sometimes Veterans don't recognize the skills they have and also don't articulate them well to translate to the civilian side.
  - On the civilian side, they may have preconceptions and stereotypes about military skills. For example, many people believe that military leaders use an authoritarian leadership style like Patton, which is usually not true these days.
  - Therefore, leadership is a valuable skill: many military people have experienced so many different situations that they learn a lot and there is an amazing array of leadership styles.
  - A lot of collaboration and teamwork to get the jobs done.
  - Innovation: this is the result of the last conflict being tactical and lower-level people-driven. These lower-level people needed to figure out a lot of problems on their own; *not* driven from the top such as countering IED devices, the Google Earth example, etc.
  - Very high comfort level with turbulent, high velocity environment: comfort with complexity.
  - Moral integrity and ethics: over the course of the last 10 years, the military has developed a focus on this; centered on professional Soldiers and leaders who had to take the higher ground.

Some Additional Online Resources

www.military.com/veteran-jobs/skills-translator
www.onetonline.org/crosswalk/MOC
www.showyourstripes.org/veterans/job-skills-translator.html
www.careerinfonet.org/MOC
www.veteranjobs.stripes.com/resources/militaryskillstranslatorform.asp
www.careerinfonet.org/moc
www.militaryconnection.com/military-skills-translator

INDEX

AARs *see* after-action reviews
Abou-Zeid, E. 67
absorptive capacity 12, 26, 73, 75, 92, 115
accountability 43, 91
acculturation 99, 141
achievement orientation 56
adaptability 56, 58, 60, 116, 118, 144, 146; *see also* flexibility
adhocracy culture 56, 57
adoption of innovations 134–135
Afghanistan conflict 29–30; culture 53, 59, 60, 62–63; knowledge corruption 82–84; leadership 46–47; structures and processes 109, 119–121; technologies 123, 125, 133, 137; training and socialization 91–92, 102, 103–104
after-action reviews (AARs) 28, 29, 89, 100–101, 106–109, 114; businesses 141–142; databases 126; knowledge corruption 71, 81; tacit knowledge sharing 9, 120–121
agility 115
AI *see* artificial intelligence
Al-Alawi, A. I. 72
Al-Baghdadi, Abu Bakr 21
Al-Marzooqi, N. Y. 72
Alony, I. 73, 75
Amazon.com 22
ambidexterity 117
Ambrosini, V. 76
American Productivity and Quality Center (APQC) 110

Amidon, D. 67
analytics 128, 129
Andrews, E. 20
Apple 15, 22, 57
apprenticeships 24, 93
apps 123, 127, 128, 129, 143
APQC *see* American Productivity and Quality Center
Arab Spring 131
artificial intelligence (AI) 2, 106, 114, 117, 125, 128, 132, 136
assertiveness 146
attitudes 17, 51; knowledge corruption 78; military 20, 78, 90, 98; socialization 99
audio technologies 124, 126
automotive industry 136
autonomy 52, 115, 116–117

"bad" knowledge 14, 15–17, 22, 23, 26
Battle of Agincourt 4
Battle of the Bulge 20–21, 27, 59, 60, 79, 93
Battle of Crecy 3–4
Battle of Gettysburg 32–33
behaviors 52–53
Berg, Z. 67
Berkshire Hathaway 39
Berkun, S. 14
Best Buy 96
big data 128
Billsberry, J. 76
Black & Decker Corp. 36, 38

Index **149**

boot camps 8, 72, 89–91, 95, 98, 99, 140–141
boundary-spanners 12, 73, 75–76
brands 50
Brexit 22
Bronowski, Jacob 65
Browaeys, M. J. 3
Brown, Joshua viii
Brubeck, Dave 94
Buffett, Warren 38–39
business-to-business (B2B) marketing 129

Cable, D. M. 99
camaraderie 53
Cameron, K. S. 56
capabilities 115–116, 117, 118
Carlzon, Jan 52
Casperson, Sam 66
Cavusgil, S. 3
Cervélo 18–19
Challenger space shuttle disaster 65–67, 70, 77, 105–106
Chamberlain, Joshua 32–33
Charvat, Mylea 139
chat systems 124, 127
chatbots 132
Cheong, M. 37
CHG Healthcare Services 96–97
Chiarelli, Peter 67
Christensen, Sean viii
CIS *see* Community Innovation Survey
clan culture 56–57
cloud technologies 127–128, 133
codified knowledge 9, 10, 24, 82; *see also* explicit knowledge
cohesion 53, 56, 58, 63, 72, 91
Cokins, Gary 15
collaboration: APQC 110; collaborative innovation 117; culture of 21, 25, 63, 96, 139; knowledge creation 24; organizational agility 115; organizational structure 116; reward-incentive system 43; SMEs 26; social capital 99; tacit knowledge sharing 76; technologies 127, 143; 3M 18, 19, 118; training and socialization 97, 141; Veterans' perspectives 147
"collective wisdom" 117
collectivist cultures 76
combination 24, 25
communication: breakdowns in 66; culture 56; effective 65; environmental turbulence 75; explicit knowledge 9;

knowledge corruption 66, 69; leadership 47, 139–140; military situations 46–47, 61–62, 78, 81–82, 92, 103–104, 118–120, 124, 145, 146; organizational structure 116–117; reward-incentive system 43; skills demanded by business 144; SMEs 26; structures and processes 114; tacit knowledge 71, 76; technologies 122, 123–130; training and socialization 95
Community Innovation Survey (CIS) 25–26
CompanyCommander.com 126–127
competition 16, 56, 57
competitive advantage 5, 8, 9–10, 25–26, 140; collaborative innovation 117; culture 50, 59; dynamic capabilities 116; knowledge management 23; SMEs 26; 3M 18, 19; training and socialization 95, 97, 141
complacency 16, 17, 65
confidence 146
conflict 38, 95
Confucius 87
context 54, 58
contingency theories of leadership 34–35
creative abrasion 12, 24
credibility 42, 140; adoption of innovations 135; military situations 29, 44, 60, 61, 82, 104, 107; tacit knowledge sharing 75–76, 79
critical thinking 144, 145, 146
cross-training 93, 98
culture 17, 21, 50–64, 139–140, 143; adoption of innovations 135; behaviors 52–53; continual learning 26; dynamic 115; enablers and blockers 54–55; importance of 51; knowledge corruption 66, 67, 69; leadership 33, 35, 37, 42; military 60–63, 72, 83, 90–91; outcomes 52; in practice 58–60; RadioShack 7; structures and processes 118; tacit knowledge sharing 12, 72, 74–76; training and socialization 95–96, 97; types of 56–58
Cummings, David 50
Cunningham, John 36
customer service 52, 55, 94
cyber security 127, 130

Data General 36
databases 114, 122, 126, 128; automotive industry 136; codified knowledge 10;

150 Index

effective 143; knowledge repositories 125, 127; military 107, 123, 126, 137; user-friendly 134
debriefings 104, 106–107, 109, 120
decentralization 116, 117
decision-making 73, 144, 145; leadership 37–38, 45, 46–47; military situations 81, 92–93, 101, 146–147
Deming, W. Edwards 34
Dexter Shoe Company 39
Dhanaraj, C. 75
diffusion of innovation 134–135
digital convergence 136
"digital Darwinism" 132–133
discovery skills 37
discussion forums 124
diversity 51
Dodge, Wagner 41
Drucker, Peter 17
Dyer, J. 37
dynamic capabilities 115–116, 118

Eastman Kodak 16–17
efficiency 56, 57–58, 117, 118
Einstein, Albert 122
email 71, 114, 119, 124, 125, 126
Emery, Tyler viii–ix
empathy 46
employees: autonomy 116–117; culture 52, 55, 56–57, 140; storytelling 55; training and socialization 52, 94, 95–99
empowerment 42, 47, 60
Enron 51
environmental scanning 18
environmental turbulence 74–75, 115, 147
ethics 147
expectations 42, 43, 45, 55
experiential interactions 24
explicit knowledge 2, 9–10, 24, 25, 66, 69; see also codified knowledge
externalization 24, 25

Facebook 8, 131, 132
Fawcett, B. 40
Felin, T. 116
Fiedler, F. E. 35
Fields, D. 75
flexibility 26, 115; culture 52, 56, 139; leadership 33; military situations 20, 60, 146; organizational structure 116; skills demanded by business 144; socialization 58; see also adaptability

Fortune 500 list of Most Admired Corporations 33
Fry, Nathan ix
fusion 24

Gauthier, Keith ix
General Motors 58
"generative-sensing capabilities" 116
geographic innovation 22
Gino, F. 55
Global Information Grid 126
Global War on Terror (GWOT) 28–30; culture 61–63; knowledge corruption 78, 80–84; leadership 45–47; structures and processes 118–121; technologies 136–137; training and socialization 101–104; see also Afghanistan conflict; Iraq War
goals: culture 51, 57, 58; leadership 35, 139, 142; reward-incentive system 43; socialization 55; tacit knowledge sharing 12, 76
Goldman Sachs 57
"good" knowledge 14, 17–19, 22
Google 57, 136
Google Earth 63, 133, 147
Green Berets 90
Greenblatt, Mark 53
"groupthink" 5, 72
Gupta, A. 2
GWOT *see* Global War on Terror

Hallinan, J. T. 39
Harkema, S. J. M. 3
Hawking, Stephen 14, 34
health care 96–97, 128
Hemphill, J. K. 34–35
Hewlett Packard (HP) 55
hierarchy culture 56, 57–58
"hip pocket" classes 104
hiring 24
Hoffer, Eric 143
Holste, J. 75
"hot wash" 29, 104, 106–107
Huang, C. 131
humbleness 21, 42, 44, 45, 145

IBM 15, 36, 58, 128
identity 99
improvised explosive devices (IEDs) 18, 30, 82, 83, 109, 120, 133, 147
incentives 33, 43, 54, 114, 117, 139, 142
individualistic cultures 76

Index **151**

information management 2
infrastructure 99–100; *see also* structures
innovation 9–10, 12, 33–34, 118;
   adhocracy culture 56, 57; Apple 15;
   collaborative 117; culture of 37, 50, 52,
   58, 59, 115, 139, 143; decision-making
   38; definitions of 3, 14–15; diffusion
   of 134–135; environmental turbulence
   74–75; Google 136; knowledge
   management 143; leadership 35, 36–37,
   38; military 20, 147; organizational
   structure 116; Salesforce.com 8; SMEs
   26; social capital 99; 3M 18, 19, 118;
   training and socialization 58, 97;
   types of 22
Instagram 132
intellectual capital 3, 98
internalization 24, 25
Internet 10, 99–100, 123, 126
Internet of Things (IoT) 128, 129–130,
   135–136
intuition 18, 23, 45, 88, 92–93, 100, 101
investopedia 35
IoT *see* Internet of Things
Ipe, M. 76
Iraq War 18, 23, 28–29; "bad" knowledge
   17, 23; culture 53, 61–62; knowledge
   capture 108; knowledge corruption
   78, 81–82; knowledge transfer 83;
   leadership 39–40, 45–46; structures and
   processes 118–119; tacit knowledge
   8, 9; technologies 136; training and
   socialization 93, 101–103
ISIS 21

Janeway, W. 115
Jobs, Steve 15, 35–36
Jones, K. 75
Jones, N. B. 67

Kaplan, J. 54–55
key leader engagement (KLE) 62
Kidder, Tracy 36, 38
Kikoski, C. K. 9
Kikoski, J. F. 9
Kiron, D. 130
KLE *see* key leader engagement
knowledge 1–3; "bad" 14, 15–17, 22,
   23, 26; decay 77; definition of 2;
   "discovered" 4; "good" 14, 17–19, 22;
   illusion of 16–17; military situations
   4–6, 8, 19–21, 27–30; new 24, 68–69,
   76, 92, 93, 99, 109, 114; RadioShack 7;

retention of 77; *see also* tacit
   knowledge
knowledge capture 2–3, 67; "generative-
   sensing capabilities" 116; military
   situations 108; structures and processes
   109, 114; tacit knowledge 68, 74;
   technologies 122, 143
knowledge corruption 58, 65–86, 142;
   causes of 66–67; deliberate 66, 67, 70;
   knowledge management challenges
   76–77; in practice 79; transfer challenges
   71–74; Veterans' perspectives 79–84
knowledge creation 8, 12, 24; "collective
   wisdom" 117; military situations 29–30,
   108; structures and processes 114;
   technologies 128, 136; 3M 18, 19; *see
   also* knowledge, new
knowledge hoarding 68, 69, 70, 77,
   94, 142
knowledge management 9–10, 23–24,
   143; challenges 76–77; definition of
   2–3; in practice 26–27; Sears 16
knowledge maps 10, 25
knowledge overload 70, 71
knowledge portals 105–106, 114
knowledge repositories 125, 127
knowledge spiral 24, 25
knowledge transfer/sharing 3, 8, 24–26,
   66; APQC 110; culture 53, 58, 59,
   62–63, 96, 139; cyber security 130;
   digital convergence 136; knowledge
   corruption 68–74, 83; leadership 33,
   37, 40, 45, 139, 142; market culture
   57; military situations 20, 92, 102, 103,
   107, 118–121; organizational structure
   116; rewards and incentives 142;
   social media 126–127; socialization 99;
   structures and processes 109, 114; tacit
   knowledge 9–11, 12, 67, 68–69, 71–72,
   74–76, 79, 120–121; technologies 122,
   124, 127, 142–143; 3M 18–19; trust 58
Knowlen, Charles ix
Korean War 27; culture 59, 60;
   knowledge corruption 79; leadership
   44; training and socialization 93, 100

La Brie, Robert E. ix
Lambe, P. 74
Landes, Barbara 50
language skills 146
Lazarova, I. 2
leadership 12, 19, 32–49, 139–140, 142;
   culture and 50, 51, 55; definitions

152 Index

of 34, 35; Enron 51; key leader engagement 62; organizational agility 115; in practice 42–43; resources 43–44; skills demanded by business 144; Veterans' perspectives 44–47, 60–61, 82, 145, 147; willingness to learn 17
learning: continual 22, 25–26, 45, 61, 75, 95–96, 98, 115, 118, 135, 139, 143; from failure 47; military situations 22, 23; structures and processes 118; tacit knowledge sharing 76; willingness to learn 17
Ledford, B. 67
Leonard-Barton, Dorothy 24, 117
Leonard, L. 75
Levie, Aaron 122
LinkedIn 132
longbow 3–4
loyalty 57
Lucey, Paul ix
Lutz, A. 16
Lyytinen, K. 135–136

Mabry, R. 94
Maginot Line 4–5
Mahon, J. F. 67
management 7
Mann Gulch forest fire 40–41
Marine Corps Center for Lessons Learned (MCCLL) 107, 119
market culture 56, 57
Maurer, Tracey 87
MCCLL *see* Marine Corps Center for Lessons Learned
McDaniel, J. 2
McGuinness, D. L. 110
McNamara, P. 98–99
media 51
medics 93–94
mentoring 24, 47, 60; clan culture 56, 57; military situations 44, 45, 102; structures and processes 114; training and socialization 93, 95, 97, 98, 99
"mesofacts" 77
Microsoft 132
military situations 3–6, 19–21, 22–23, 27–30; "bad" knowledge 17, 23; culture 52–54, 59, 60–63; intuition 18; knowledge corruption 70–71, 78, 79–84; leadership 32–33, 39–40, 44–47; structures and processes 106–109, 118–121; tacit knowledge 8, 9–10; team cohesion 140; technologies

123, 124–125, 126–127, 133, 136–137, 142–143; training and socialization 52, 72–73, 87–94, 98, 100–104, 107, 109, 120, 140, 141–142; translation of skills to business 144–147
Miller, Joseph ix
mission 19, 58; environmental turbulence 75; leadership 33, 42, 139, 142; reward-incentive system 43; tacit knowledge sharing 12, 76; training and socialization 95, 140–141
mobile technologies 124, 125, 128–129, 132, 133, 143
Mohammed, Y. F. 72
Moore, B. 90
moral integrity 147
Morgan, J. 135
motivation 56, 72, 91, 94, 144
Munger, Charlie 39
Murphy, Matthew ix
"muscle memory" 8, 88, 92, 95, 101, 146

Nagy, C. 90
nano-technology 18–19
network innovation 15
networks 24, 71–72; boundary-spanners 73, 75–76; military technologies 126; social 25, 56, 72, 75, 140; technologies 122–123, 135–136, 143
9/11 terrorist attacks 66, 123
Nitzsche, P. 26
Nonaka, I. 24, 25
Nordstrom 52
norms: culture 51, 56, 58, 135; knowledge corruption 66, 69; military 72, 91; socialization 78, 99; storytelling 73, 74
Noy, N. F. 110

ontologies 110, 112–113, 114
O'Reilly, C. A. 52, 117
organizational agility 115
organizational design 116, 117
organizational structure 115–117
Osterwalder, A. 51, 54, 56
"outcomes-based training" 102

Panahi, S. 74
Parlby, D. 3
participation 56, 57
partnerships 54–55
Perez-Soltero, A. 26
personalities 63, 70, 80
Peters, Tom 15, 32

Phys.org 133
Plato 34
PME *see* professional military education
"point papers" 119
political–social innovation 22
polyarchy 116
positive attitude 43, 144
Powell, T. C. 116
power 58, 116, 139
Power, Daniel J. 15
process innovation 22, 25–26
processes 21, 105–121; knowledge portal
106; lessons learned 114; military
106–109, 118–121; in practice 118;
taxonomies and ontologies 110–113;
theory 115–117
product innovation 22
professional military education (PME) 119
professionalism 144, 146

Quinn, R. E. 56

R&D *see* research and development
RadioShack 6–7
recipient blindness 76–77
rehearsals 104
relationships: culture 25, 58, 59; leadership
35, 37, 42, 140; military situations 62,
63; Salesforce.com 8; social media 130;
tacit knowledge sharing 12, 74, 75; 3M
19; training and socialization 95, 97,
140–141
relative advantage 135
reputation 57, 75–76, 140
research and development (R&D) 24, 36
resources 26, 115
respect 33, 42, 45, 59, 139, 142
responsibility 43, 53–54, 61, 72, 91, 102
rewards 33, 43, 96, 114, 142
Rhodes, Ann 50
Rhodes, Cecil 34
Rijal, S. 74–75
risk 115
risk-taking 19, 50, 56, 57, 139
Ritz-Carlton Hotel 55, 94, 95, 114
Roberts, P. 132
Rogers, Everett M. 134
Rossignol, Norman ix–x
rules 54, 57
Ryazanova, O. 98–99

Salesforce.com 8, 54–55
SALUTE 102

Savonix 139
Scandinavian Airlines (SAS) 52
scenarios 146
Schultz, Howard 50, 55
Schumpeter, Joseph Alois 32
SCT *see* social cognitive theory
Sears 16, 22
security 127, 130
sensing 115, 116, 117, 118
servant leadership 35, 42
sexual harassment 51, 87
shadowing 83, 120
shared meaning 59, 71, 78, 79,
92–93, 141
Shirland, Jeffery x
Skyrme, D. 67
slack.com 128
small and medium size enterprises
(SMEs) 26
smartphones 7, 8, 124, 125, 130
Snapchat 131, 132
social capital 98, 99
social cognitive theory (SCT) 135
social media 74, 114, 117, 124, 126–127,
130–133, 143
social networks 25, 56, 72, 75, 140
social proof 117
socialization 12, 78, 87–104, 109, 141;
culture 52–53, 55, 58; definition
of 97–98; knowledge spiral 24, 25;
military 72, 87–94, 100–104; in
practice 100; Salesforce.com 8; tacit
knowledge sharing 72; theory 97–99
software 123, 125, 126, 128, 143
Solis, B. 132–133
SOPs *see* standard operating procedures
Sørensen, J. 56
Soto, V. L. 26
Special Forces 90, 102
Stalin, Joseph 40
Standard and Poor's (S&P) 500 Index 16, 39
standard operating procedures (SOPs) 119
Stanley Works 36
Starbucks 55
storytelling 55, 73–74
stress 146
structures 21, 99–100, 105–121, 142;
lessons learned 114; military 106–109,
118–121; in practice 118; taxonomies
and ontologies 110–113; theory
115–117
Sullenberger, Chesley 41
Sweeney, Brigid 16

154 Index

Swoboda, Joseph x
symbolic capital 98

tacit knowledge 2, 24–25; definition of
9; knowledge spiral 25; Mann Gulch
forest fire 41; military situations 8, 60,
72–73, 107, 120–121; social media 124;
storytelling 73–74; transfer of 9–11, 12,
67, 68–69, 71–72, 74–76, 79, 120–121
tactical operations centers (TOCs) 71, 81,
118–119
Takeuchi, N. 24, 25
Talwar, R. 2
task focused leadership 35, 47
Tauber, Todd 87
taxonomies 110–113, 114
Taylor, R. 3
teams: clan culture 57; decision-
making 38; leadership 33, 42, 140;
self-organizing 116; size of 37; tacit
knowledge sharing 12; teamwork 95,
144, 145, 146, 147; trust 75
technology 21, 122–138, 142–143;
changes in 2; communication 122,
123–130; diffusion of innovation
134–135; Eastman Kodak 16–17;
Internet of Things 128, 129–130,
135–136; knowledge portal 106; lessons
learned 133; nano-technology 18–19;
opportunities and threats 115; SMEs
26; Technology Acceptance Model
135; see also social media
Teece, D. 115, 117
telephones 124, 125, 126
terrorism: ISIS 21; 9/11 terrorist
attacks 66, 123; see also Global War on
Terror
3M 18–19, 22, 57, 118
TOCs see tactical operations centers
Tolstoy, Leo 65
Tour de France 18
training 24, 78, 87–104, 109, 140–142;
communication 47, 120; culture 55;
knowledge corruption 69; knowledge
portal 106; lessons learned 97; military
72–73, 80, 87–94, 98, 100–104, 107,
109, 120, 140, 141–142; in practice
100; Salesforce.com 8; SMEs 26;
structures and processes 118; theory
97–99; types of 95–97
Trantopoulos, K. 25–26
trust: adoption of innovations 135;
collectivist cultures 76; culture 19,

25, 58, 59; environmental turbulence
75; knowledge corruption 78, 80;
leadership 33, 37, 42, 45, 140, 142;
military situations 28, 54, 61, 72, 93;
Salesforce.com 8; social media 130;
tacit knowledge sharing 12, 74, 75, 76;
training and socialization 93, 97, 141
TurboTax 109
Tushman, M. L. 52, 117
Twain, Mark 17
Twitter 8, 131
"Type A" personalities 63

Uber 58
uncertainty 56, 115, 117
Undiscovered Maine 111–112
United Kingdom 22
United States Army 53, 58, 81, 83, 102;
see also military situations; Veterans
United States Marine Corps 81, 83;
culture 51, 53, 63; structures and
processes 106–109, 119; training and
socialization 72–73, 90–91, 99, 100,
141; see also military situations;
Veterans
United States Strategic Command 20

values: boot camp training 95; culture
51, 55, 58, 115, 135; military 20,
72, 91; social cognitive theory 135;
socialization 55, 98, 99; storytelling 73;
tacit knowledge sharing 76
Veterans 18, 22–23, 27–30; "bad"
knowledge 17; culture 53–54, 59,
60–63; knowledge corruption 70–71,
78, 79–84; leadership 39–40, 42,
44–47, 142; structures and processes
108–109, 118–121; technologies
136–137; training and socialization 72,
88–90, 91, 92–93, 100–104; translation
of skills to business 144–147; see also
military situations
video technologies 124, 125, 132
Vietnam War 23, 27–28; culture 59,
60–61; knowledge corruption 79–80;
leadership 44–45, 62, 82; training and
socialization 88–89, 100–101
vision 19, 23, 28, 58; environmental
turbulence 75; leadership 33, 42,
139; reward-incentive system 43;
tacit knowledge sharing 12;
training and socialization 95,
140–141

Voskamp, Ann 87
Vroom, V. 37–38

Walmart 22
Walt Disney Corporation 51, 55
Waterman, Robert 15
Watson 128
weak ties 73
Whitford, D. 8
Wong, J. 132

World War I 4
World War II 4–6, 20–21, 27; culture 59, 60; knowledge corruption 79; leadership 44; standard operating procedures 119; technologies 124; training and socialization 52–53, 80, 93, 100

Yetton, P. 37–38

Zaccaro, S. J. 34